# Idaho's Payette River Railroads: History Through the Miles

Barton Jennings

**Idaho's Payette River Railroads: History Through the Miles**
Copyright © 2020 by Barton Jennings

All rights reserved. This book may not be duplicated or transmitted in any way, or stored in an information retrieval system, without the express written consent of the publisher, except in the form of brief excerpts or quotations for the purpose of review. Making copies of this book, or any portion, for any purpose other than your own, is a violation of United States copyright laws.

**Publisher's Cataloging-in-Publication Data**
Jennings, Barton

Idaho's Payette River Railroads: History Through the Miles
176p.; 21cm.
ISBN: 978-1-7327888-3-1

Library of Congress Control Number: 2020942453

First Edition

Front cover photo by Barton Jennings. Tunnel No. 3, MP 38.5.
Back cover photo by Sarah Jennings.

Please send comments or corrections to sarah@techscribes.com

TechScribes, Inc.
PO Box 620
Avon, IL 61415
www.techscribes.com

Printed in the United States of America

# Contents

Preface ..................................................................... 5
History of Idaho's Payette River Railroads ..................... 9
**The Payette Branch** .................................................. 15
**Idaho Northern Branch** ............................................ 43
Nampa to Maddens ..................................................... 55
   Union Pacific Idaho Northern Industrial Lead
Maddens to Emmett .................................................... 67
   Abandoned
Emmett to Cascade ..................................................... 79
   Idaho Northern & Pacific
Cascade to McCall ..................................................... 157
   Abandoned
About the Author ...................................................... 175

## Other books by Barton Jennings

### History Through the Miles

*Arkansas & Missouri Railroad: History Through the Miles*
*Alaska Railroad: History Through the Miles*
*Iowa Interstate Railroad: History Through the Miles*
*Everett Railroad: History Through the Miles*
*Tennessee Central Railway: History Through the Miles*
*Whitewater Valley Railroad: History Through the Miles*
*Oregon's Joseph Branch: History Through the Miles*
*Missouri & North Arkansas Railroad: History Through the Miles*
*Hennepin Canal Parkway: History Through the Miles*

### Textbooks

*The Basics of Transportation: Policies, Practices and Pricing – An Applied Perspective*

# Preface

Idaho is not a state that many people think about when discussing historic rail lines. Instead, it is thought of as a state of mountains, mining and timber. However, these natural resources are why trains were a major part of the state's history.

The United States acquired much of the land which eventually became Idaho when Thomas Jefferson negotiated the Louisiana Purchase in 1803. At that time, few whites had ever visited the region and few Americans had any idea what the land was like. The first visitors were trappers chasing the last of the beaver pelts, following reports from Lewis and Clark, who spent time in the area between 1804 and 1806. Many of the mountains and rivers in northern Idaho were named during that exploration. Central Idaho was heavily explored after the discovery of gold in the area from 1861 to 1863. The first railroad entered Idaho in 1874 at Franklin (also the first permanent settlement, founded in 1860) in the southeast part of the state.

The history of the name Idaho is an interesting one. George M. Willing created the name Idaho for the new territory of the Pikes' Peak region – Colorado. At the time, Indian words were popular and Willing came up with the name to sound Indian. After Congress discovered that the word wasn't Indian, Colorado was chosen instead for the territory. However, the word had taken up use in the Columbia, Clearwater and Salmon River areas. In 1862, the first large mineral discoveries in the area were given the name Idaho Mines. The acceptance of the name led to the creation and naming of the Idaho Territory (today's states of Idaho, Montana and Wyoming) by President Lincoln in 1863.

The Idaho Territory was not always popular with politicians. Between 1863 and 1890, the Idaho Territory had 16 governors, four whom never set foot in Idaho. Idaho achieved statehood on July 3, 1890, as the 43rd state. Today, Idaho is the 14th largest state at 83,557 square miles and has a population of about 1.2 million, 41st in the country. Boise is the only city with a population of more than 100,000. Idaho leads the nation in the production of potatoes, lentils, Austrian winter peas, and trout (85% of all commercial trout). Many of the crops are grown along the Payette Branch of the railroad. North of Emmett on the Idaho Northern Branch, most of the land is National Forest – sixty-three percent of Idaho is public land managed by the federal government. The Frank Church River of No Return Wilderness area, located just east of Cascade, is the largest wilderness area in the 48 contiguous states with 2.3 million acres.

The railroads up the Payette River Valley operated over some of the most scenic and isolated country in North America. Built to move apples and other farm products, and then timber for the sawmills and livestock, the rail lines often operated in obscurity. Union Pacific eventually controlled the lines and coordinated their operations with the needs of the sawmills, as well as the mainline trains that would haul the products to market. The Idaho Northern Branch received some fame when excursion passenger trains operated over parts of the scenic route 1998-2015. However, the route is still essentially unknown to most people across the country.

This route description was first written in 2002-2003 for a charter trip that the author operated over the railroad from Payette to Cascade on August 8, 2003. Because of the many requests for copies of the trip handout, a decision was made to release it as part of the *History Through the Miles* series of books. Most of the photos come from this 2003 charter as we made more than a dozen stops to explore facilities and to photograph the train and features along the line. With new information, and the many changes that have happened since the charter train, the route description has been updated and added to. Much of the information comes from internal railroad records, government and public records, railroad workers, and conversations with old and new friends. Some of the information comes from the author's own personal notes from several explorations over the line, and from his time working for Union Pacific on the Northwestern District.

Directions on this railroad will be based upon the railroad's own terminology. A train heading from Payette toward Cascade is heading railroad-north. Note that every station and bridge location is identified by a milepost location. Railroads identify locations along their routes by mileposts, much like highways do. For the Payette Branch and Idaho Northern Branch, the mileposts date back to the construction of the railroads. The mileposts for each location are included in this guide. There are signs every mile along the railroad that identify this distance, so watch for them if you wish. Hopefully this book will be of assistance in some ways – *Idaho's Payette River Railroads: History Through the Miles*.

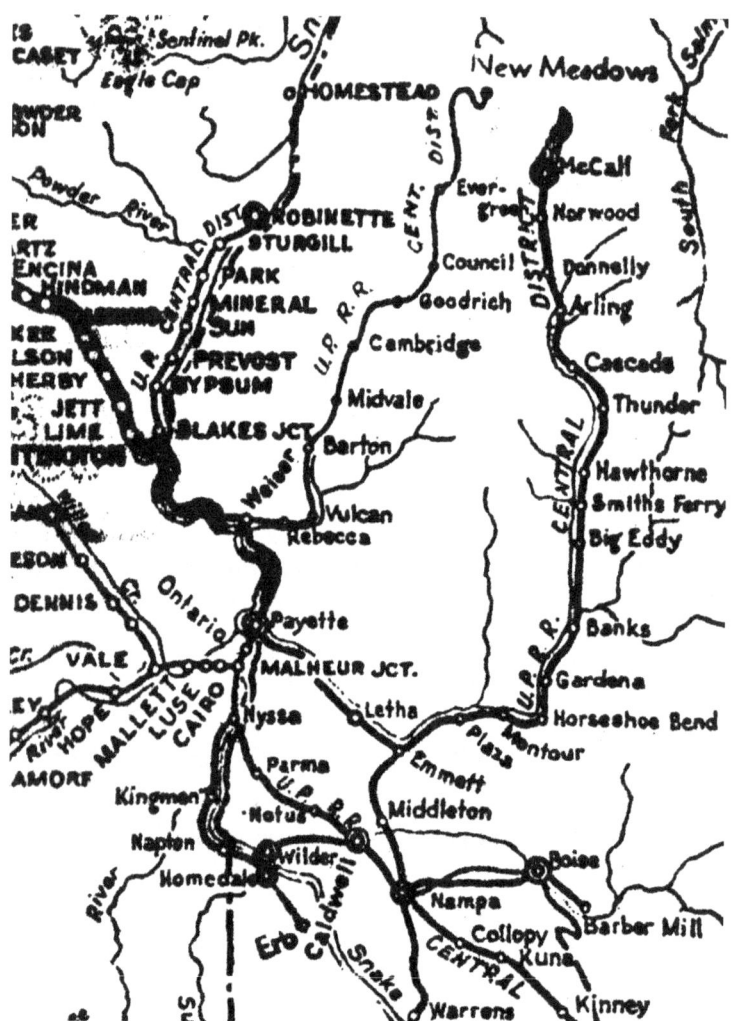

*Time-Table No. 27*, Effective Sunday, June 28, 1942. Union Pacific Railroad Company, Northwestern District, Oregon Division, Map.

# History of Idaho's Payette River Railroads
## The Payette and Idaho Northern Branches

The railroads of the Payette River Valley were built by a number of companies, including the Payette Valley Railroad, the Payette Valley Extension Railroad, the Idaho Northern Railway, and the Oregon Short Line. These railroads all seemed to have had great plans that would have developed the lands they passed through, and made their owners rich from hauling the products they produced. They certainly did change the territory, supporting the timbering industry and helping farms and orchards to develop.

All of the lines eventually became owned by the Oregon Short Line, and then Union Pacific Railroad. The Oregon Short Line invested in these lines, and even expanded them. For Union Pacific, the Idaho Northern Branch (Nampa-McCall) and the Payette Branch (Payette-Emmett) were feeder lines to the mainline of the Northwestern District. The branches were operated individually, with some coordination at their junction at Emmett.

For a number of years, mixed trains ran regularly over both lines, serving sawmills, farms, and the few passengers along the railroad. As the timber was cut, traffic volumes decreased, and the line from Cascade to McCall was abandoned on May 14, 1980.

In 1993, the lines were leased or sold to the Idaho Northern & Pacific, a subsidiary of the Rio Grande Pacific Corporation. The difficult route from Emmett to Nampa was not needed by the Idaho Northern & Pacific, and soon abandoned. This combined the Payette Branch (Payette-Emmett) and Idaho Northern Branch (Emmett-Cascade) as a single route between the mountain community of Cascade, and the Union Pacific mainline near the farming community of Payette. Other changes have been caused by the closure of several major sawmills, and a movement toward tourism and away from the use of local natural resources for mining and timber.

Because of the different stories and histories, information about the various routes and companies are presented in greater detail with the description of each line. Note that some stations are marked with a code, such as Emmett (MF). The code is the station's telegraph or agent's code. As stations were consolidated, and agencies were closed, fewer and fewer stations were assigned such a code. Those used in this book are from the *Union Pacific System List of Officers, Agencies, Stations, Etc. No. 60*, dated January 1, 1930.

## Idaho Northern & Pacific Railroad Company

Today, the Payette and Idaho Northern Branches are operated by the Idaho Northern & Pacific. The Idaho Northern & Pacific (INPR) acquired their lines in western Idaho and eastern Oregon from Union Pacific on November 15, 1993. The company is a subsidiary of Rio Grande Pacific Corporation (RGP). Rio Grande Pacific owns and operates four shortline railroads in six states (Idaho Northern & Pacific Railroad; Nebraska Central Railroad; New Orleans & Gulf Coast Railway; Wichita, Tillman & Jackson Railway) which haul more than 70,000 carloads of freight annually. They total more than 700 miles in length and serve approximately 140 freight customers. Each railroad provides badly needed rail service which saves and creates jobs for the local economies.

Lumber has historically represented the majority of the products shipped on the Idaho line, although sand, agricultural products and chemicals are also moved, but with no regular shippers north of Emmett as this is being written. For a number of years (1998-2015), the Idaho Northern & Pacific also saw the operation of the Thunder Mountain Line, a scenic excursion railroad operation which operated 2½-hour trips out of Horseshoe Bend (15 miles to Banks) and Cascade (16 miles to Smiths Ferry). The passenger train also handled rafters on some trips since the Payette River is a heavily used rafting river.

The INPR initially acquired the Payette River Valley railroads through both purchase and lease. The routes **purchased** included (1) the Payette Branch from MP 0.39 at Payette, ID, to MP 27.0 at Emmett, ID; and (2) the Idaho Northern Branch from MP 28.0 at Emmett, ID, to MP 99.68 at Cascade, ID. The INPR **leased** (1) the Payette Branch from MP 27.0 to MP 29.1 at Emmett, ID; and (2) the Idaho Northern Branch from MP 5.0 at Maddens, ID, to MP 28.0 at Emmett, ID. **Trackage rights** were obtained on the Idaho Northern Branch between MP 0.00 at Nampa, ID, and MP 5.00 at Maddens, ID.

The Idaho Northern & Pacific actually was created out of a number of other lines. This included the **New Meadows Branch** in Idaho. This route included trackage rights on the New Meadows Branch between MP 0.00 and MP 1.0 at Weiser, ID; and on the Union Pacific mainline between MP 519.0 at Weiser, ID, and MP 454.0 at Nampa, ID. INPR also purchased the New Meadows Branch from MP 1.0 at Weiser, ID, to MP 84.55 at Rubicon, ID. There was little business on the New Meadows Branch and the Interstate Commerce Commission approved its abandonment on November 1, 1995, and the last freight train operated on November 18, 1995. The rails were removed during the summer of 1996.

In Oregon, the INPR also took over the **Joseph Branch** out of La Grande. This included leased track from MP 0.0 at LaGrande, OR, to MP 21.0 at Elgin, OR; and purchase of the line from MP 21.0 at Elgin, OR, to MP 83.58 at Joseph, OR. The Idaho Northern & Pacific now operates La Grande to Elgin, and has sold the line from Elgin to Joseph to the Wallowa Union Railroad Authority. The book *Oregon's Joseph Branch: History Through the Miles*, covers this former Union Pacific branchline.

It did not take long for the Idaho Northern & Pacific to present a clear image to the shippers along the line, featuring their cream and forest green paint scheme. Here, caboose #049 is parked at Emmett, Idaho. This caboose was built in March 1967 as Union Pacific 25604 (Class CA-9) by the International Car Company of Kenton, Ohio. Photo by Barton Jennings.

The Idaho Northern & Pacific operates what are generally very clean locomotives, featuring their saw blade emblem, as shown on IN&P #4506. Photo by Barton Jennings.

*Idaho's Payette River Railroads: History Through the Miles*

# The Payette Branch

## The Payette Branch

The former Union Pacific Payette Branch, operating between Payette and Emmett, Idaho, was actually built in two stages by two different companies. The Oregon Short Line (OSL) corporate history, completed for the federal Interstate Commerce Commission, shows the Payette Valley Railroad being started at Payette on April 27, 1906, and completed to New Plymouth, Idaho, on August 30, 1906 (10.83 miles). The Payette Valley Extension Railroad was started at New Plymouth on April 1, 1910, and completed to Emmett on October 10, 1910 (17.96 miles). This extension to Emmett connected the line to the Idaho Northern Railway, providing Emmett a second route to the OSL mainline that operated between Wyoming and Oregon.

On February 6, 1906, the **Payette Valley Railroad Company** was incorporated under the general laws of Utah. The planned construction of the Payette Valley Railroad was reported in numerous magazines across the country. Both *The Railway Age* (February 16, 1906) and *The Railway and Engineering Review* (February 17, 1906) had short articles that stated the railroad had been incorporated and that C. W. Nibley of Ogden, Utah, was president. Additionally, both stated that H. E. Dunn was vice-president and general manager, A. B. Moss was treasurer, and F. S. Murphy was secretary. While the office was listed as being at Payette, it was obvious to many that Nibley was calling the shots from Utah.

C. W. Nibley was heavily involved in land, railroads, and agricultural investments across the northwest. Charles Wilson Nibley was a Utah millionaire, and also the fifth presiding bishop of The Church of Jesus Christ of Latter-day Saints. Nibley had managed several companies owned by the church, and was an acknowledged legal mind who used many tricks to claim land, including manipulating the Homestead Act and paying off investigating government agents. His writings also showed that he loved monopolies, believing competition was an "economic waste." He had partnered with David Eccles, Utah's first multimillionaire, on trying to corner the sugar beet industry in Utah, Idaho and Oregon, and recognized the value that transportation had to the growing sugar beet industry in the area.

*The Railway and Engineering Review* article stated that the "line will tap a large beet growing region in Payette valley" while *The Railway Age* simply stated that the line would go "through a rich agricultural and fruit section." Hiram E. Dunn was apparently the local Payette representative for the railroad and was a regular item in local newspapers. He was quoted in the March 20, 1908, issue of *The Railway Age* with a proposal to extend the line seven miles from New Plymouth to Falk's Store. The 1911 *Poor's Manual of Railroads* provides some additional information about the railroad, stating that for the year ending June 30, 1910, the railroad had $8415 in passenger revenue, $8021 in freight revenue, and $997 in other revenues. It also stated that the railroad was built using rail that weighed 35 pounds per yard, and that the railroad used mixed trains, providing both freight and passenger service.

On May 25, 1910, the **Payette Valley Extension Railroad Company** was incorporated under the general laws of Utah, to expand the railroad. The May 27, 1910, issue of *Railway Age Gazette* reported that the existing railroad (Payette Valley Railroad) was "building an extension from New Plymouth, southeast to Emmett, 19 miles, under the name of the Payette Valley Extension Railroad." The article stated that the grading contract was held by the

Northwestern Engineering Company and that "eleven cars of rails and spikes are on the ground, and ties are being received. The company expects to have the line in operation to Emmett by August 1." *Moody's Manual of Railroads* (1914) stated that the Payette Valley Extension Railroad had "the same officers and stockholders, operates the same equipment and its operations are included in those of the Payette Valley Railroad." It showed that all of the debt was held by the Oregon Short Line Railroad Company. It also stated that the Payette Valley Extension Railroad was built using 52-pound rail (weight per yard), instead of the earlier 35-pound rail.

There are some reports that the Payette Valley Railroad, and later the Payette Valley Extension Railroad, never bought or operated its own rolling stock. Instead, the Oregon Short Line Railroad leased the lines and operated them as part of their larger system. However, *Poor's Manual of Railroads* (1911) stated that as of June 30, 1910, the Payette Valley Railroad had 2 locomotives, 2 passenger cars, 4 box cars, 15 flat cars, and 1 coal car.

An interesting note in the *Fifth Annual Report of the Railroad Commission of Oregon to the Governor* (December 15, 1911), showed that the Oregon Short Line had a funded debt of $140,000 involving the Payette Valley Extension Railroad Company. Other reports showed that the Oregon Short Line held $44,000 of First Mortgage bonds, payable at 5%, of the Payette Valley Railroad, and $140,000 of the Payette Valley Extension Railroad. By this time, some had called the railroads a front for E. H. Harriman's Oregon Short Line, and both railroads were sold to the Oregon Short Line on August 5, 1914.

The line basically follows the Payette River, which runs to the north of the railroad. This is farm and orchard country, which explains all of the irrigation canals that the line crosses. The Payette to Emmett line was always agricultural-based, serving part of Idaho's largest fruit-raising district, as well as thousands of acres of vegetable production. This soon led the Payette Branch to be lined with fruit and vegetable warehouses and packing plants. Although the line was relatively straight, the Payette Valley Railroad was nicknamed "The Punkin' Vine" for many years due to its vine-like route through the area's fields.

The Payette Branch was traditionally part of Union Pacific's Idaho Division, a part of the old Northwestern District. However, it was never heavily used, often limited to a daily round trip of the mixed train, with heavier operations during the fruit and vegetable packing and shipping season. In 1948, Union Pacific ran a daily except Sunday mixed train between Payette and Emmett. Eastward, it ran as train #383, leaving Payette at 7:00am and arriving at Emmett at 8:50am, averaging 16.2 miles per hour. It returned as train #384, leaving Emmett at 1:00pm and arriving at Payette at 2:45pm, running at an average of 16.8 miles per hour. The trains became #483 and #484 by the January 1, 1950, public timetable, but still operated daily except Sunday. The mixed train passenger service ended by the September 25, 1960, public timetable.

Union Pacific sold the Payette Branch to the Idaho Northern & Pacific (IN&P) as a part of a package of lines on November 15, 1993. While Union Pacific considered the line to be east-west, the Idaho Northern & Pacific considers it to be north-south, with Emmett to the north and Payette to the south. This makes a great deal of sense when it is considered that the IN&P operates the lines in the area as a Payette to Cascade operation. Today, the route from Payette to Emmett is the Payette Subdivision of the Idaho Northern & Pacific.

The telegraph code for each station, as shown in the *Union Pacific System List of Officers, Agencies, Stations, Etc.*

*No. 60*, dated January 1, 1930, is included with the station name.

0.0   **PAYETTE (AY)** – Payette is located east of the confluence of the Snake and Payette Rivers. The area has a long and interesting history, ranging from Shoshone Indian camps to fur traders to gold prospectors to railroad construction days to today's agricultural businesses. This area was used by gold miners as they traveled between the Columbia River and the gold fields of the Boise Basin. It was also a stop along the Oregon Trail, just a few miles short of Farewell Bend where the wagon trains left the Snake River lowlands and cut across the Blue Mountains on their way to the Columbia River. By 1863, Bluff Station, two miles east of Payette, was a major stop on these routes. A post office opened in the Payette area in 1864. Down river at Washoe, near where the Snake and Payette Rivers join, the Stuart brothers had established a roadhouse and ferry. Apparently, these weren't the only businesses that they were in as they were eventually run out of the county by area vigilantes. Ranching in the area boomed after 1867 when Peter Pence brought a large herd of cattle to the area from Washington State (and the Stuarts left town).

Payette was originally founded as an Oregon Short Line Railroad construction camp with the name of Boomerang in 1883, named for the log boom in the river which was used for holding railroad ties. Robert Strahorn, Union Pacific agent, chose the site for the depot and began to lay out an organized town. Reportedly, more than 250,000 railroad ties were floated down the Payette River from near Cascade, keeping the construction camp and its log boom very busy. Eventually, Boomerang was renamed Payetteville for the Payette River, which was named for Francois Payette, a French-Canadian fur trapper for the North West Company and the area's first settler in 1818. Payette was also the first postmaster at old Fort Boise, built in 1834. Legend also has it that Payette brought the first cattle to the area.

The town name was later changed to the City of Payette, incorporated in 1891. In that year, Payette hosted two general stores, two drug stores, two livery stables, two hotels, one hardware and stove store, a four-room school house, two churches, two brick plants, and the Payette Valley Bank. It also had a large sawmill and two of the largest nurseries and prune orchards in the northwest states.

Today, Payette, with a population of 7500, is the county seat of Payette County, established in 1917 after first splitting from Ada County and later Canyon County. The area produces apples, sugar beets, onions and corn from the surrounding fields and orchards. For baseball fans, Payette also produced Hall of Famer Harmon Killebrew. Payette has some competitive disadvantages to nearby Ontario, since Oregon doesn't have a sales tax. This draws a great deal of consumer business away from the community. The city is at an elevation of 2147 feet above sea level and the rail line climbs gently as it heads east toward Emmett.

## The Railroad at Payette

In 1917, the Oregon Short Line (Union Pacific) mainline was lined with fruit packing plants and warehouses as it passed through Payette. Apples were a major source of revenue for local farmers, and other fruits and vegetables were also common. Among the companies in Payette at the time were Earle Fruit Company of the Northwest, Idaho Products Company, Payette District Fruit Growers Association, Denney & Co., and Idaho Canning Company. Today, Riverfront Produce and General Produce Distributors still operate in this same area. The small rail yard on the west side of the mainline is also still active, used to serve local industries and as interchange tracks with the Idaho Northern & Pacific, the current operator of the Payette Branch.

The Oregon Short Line had a freight depot on the east side of the tracks north of 2nd Avenue North. A block further south was the passenger depot, built in line with 1st Avenue North. Both buildings are gone today, but the foundation of the depot can still be clearly seen. For many years, the station had both a day and a night operator using "AY" as the telegraph code. The station was at Milepost 502.7 on the mainline, or Milepost 0.0 of the Payette Branch.

In 1948, Union Pacific's *City of Portland* had Payette as a flag stop (westbound #105 at 11:40pm and eastbound #106 at 4:18am) while *The Idahoan* made regular daily stops (#11 at 6:55am and #12 at 8:37pm). Interestingly enough, the *Portland Rose* made a regular daily stop at Payette westbound (#17 at 5:38pm) while the eastbound train had Payette as a flag stop (#18 at 9:55am). In 1945, local mixed train #383 would leave Payette at 7:00am daily except Sunday, while #384 arrived at 2:45pm.

Payette was also once the site of a Pacific Fruit Express (PFE) icing station and natural ice plant (one of nine nationally). The facility was originally built and used by Armour but was sold to PFE on October 1, 1907, shortly after PFE was formed and a Supreme Court ruling broke up the Armour monopoly on reefer (refrigerated railroad car) service. PFE was formed to provide reefers for Union Pacific and Southern Pacific customers. The facility was used to furnish ice for initial icing for agricultural and fruit business coming from the New Meadows, New Plymouth, Payette Valley, Burns, and Brogan Branches in the area. Ice was cut from the Payette River as well as a small pond. The 29-acre icing facility (land, buildings, pond, etc.) was retired in 1923 and sold to the Palumbo-Arata Fruit Company in 1930 for $3000.

Trains leaving Payette for the Payette Branch head south (railroad-north on the branchline, railroad-east on the mainline) from the yard, cross the Payette River using a six-span through plate girder bridge, and then immediately turn east onto the branch. During the early 1900s, a track maintenance section gang was based at Payette and maintained the track to near New Plymouth.

**0.4 PAYETTE BRANCH SWITCH** – Located at the mainline Milepost of 502.7, the railroad turns east to follow the Payette River. The Idaho Northern & Pacific acquired the line starting at the clearance point of the switch. To the west is a large cattle feedlot. Almost immediately the Payette Branch passes through the operation of its first customer, TVM Recycling, a small metals scrap yard.

Not far past the scrap yard is a relatively new siding, measuring 1700 feet long.

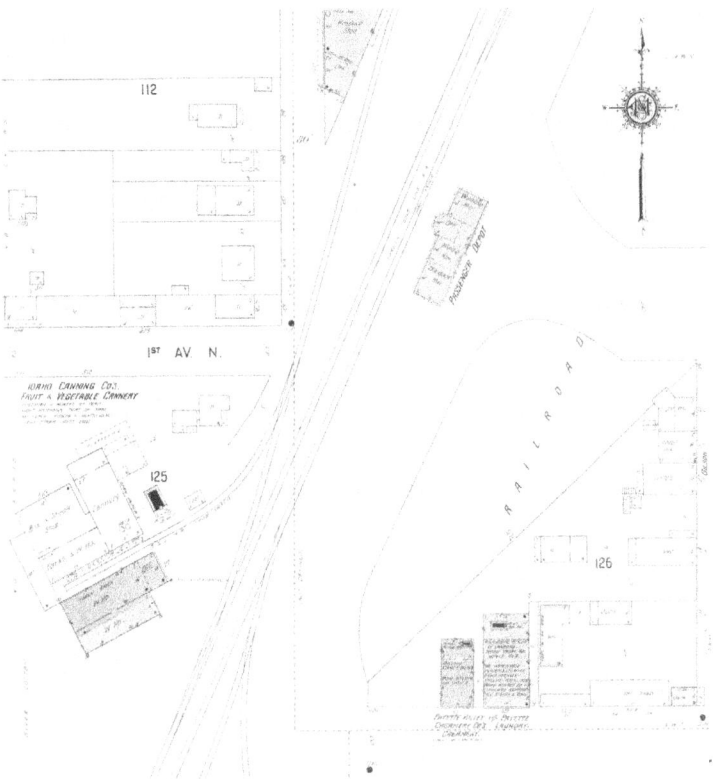

Sanborn Fire Insurance Map from Payette, Payette County, Idaho. Sanborn Map Company, Nov, 1917. Library of Congress. https://www.loc.gov/item/sanborn01653_004/.

IN&P #4506 sits in the new siding near the Payette Branch Switch with a charter passenger train in 2003. Photo by Barton Jennings.

**2.1 WASHOE DITCH BRIDGE** – The Payette area averages only eleven inches of rainfall a year, versus the national average of 38 inches. It also gets about 13 inches of snow a year. Due to the low rainfall, much of this area is irrigated using a series of canals and ditches. The water generally comes from rivers that receive mountain snow melt for much of the year. The Washoe Irrigation and Water Power Company was one of the later irrigation canal companies, but it supplied water to much of the land that was not easy to water, approximately 2200 acres.

Immediately adjacent to the railroad is the Fruitland Payette River Water Treatment Plant. This facility was greatly expanded in 1991, and has recently won awards from the Environmental Protection Agency. The plant covers five acres and has a total operating volume of eight million gallons.

**2.9** **U.S. HIGHWAY 95 BRIDGE** – This is a four-span, beam ballast deck bridge that crosses the four-lane highway. Highway 95 is a true border-to-border road, running between the Mexican border at San Luis, Arizona, and the Canadian border at Eastport, Idaho. The road is 1574 miles long.

Highway 95 was one of the original highways proposed in the 1925 Bureau of Public Roads numbering plan. However, at the time, it was designed to be built only between Payette and Eastport. By the time of the approval of the 1926 plan, the south end was at Weiser, Idaho. It was extended south to Mexico in the late 1930s.

**3.3** **INGARD** – This is a retired station from the early days of the rail line. It was located at the NW 24th Street grade crossing.

D. L. Ingard played quite a few roles in this area during the early 1900s. He operated 20 acres of apple trees and was president of the Idaho-Oregon Fruit Growers Association in 1915. He also served as a member of State Board of Horticultural Inspection for a number of years. He also founded the Fruitland State Bank in 1910 and served as its president.

**3.9** **EIFFIE** – Look for the grade crossing with North 16th Street. This is a small agricultural center located at 2206 feet above sea level, served by a short spur track into the Woodgrain Millwork facility. Woodgrain Millwork is a family-owned and operated company based in Fruitland, Idaho. The firm has manufactured wood doors, mouldings and windows since 1954. The firm has recently acquired several mills and plants in the La Grande, Oregon, area from Boise Cascade.

As the railroad heads towards Emmett and out of the Snake River valley, the railroad is in the middle of a climb of about 0.5% that lasts for about one mile. The railroad is also heading due south at this location. During the 1940s, there was a 20-car siding here, with Eiffie as a flag stop for trains #383 and #384, with the eastbound train at 7:10am and the westbound train at 2:30pm.

4.3    FARMER'S CO-OP CANAL BRIDGE – Crossed on a three-span timber pile trestle, this canal runs from north of Fruitland to south of Little Rock and is a major irrigation canal for the valley.

5.1    FRUITLAND (FR) – It is hard to imagine today, as the railroad passes through fields of mint, alfalfa, and other field crops, that this area was once covered with apple orchards. Apples were an early crop, and getting these apples to the national market was a big reason for the construction of the Payette Valley Railroad.

John Hall homesteaded the area in 1897, acquiring 160 acres. He sold half to Anthony and Amelia Zeller, who platted the town in 1908, with it known as Zeller's Crossing. Fruit was already growing in the area, and one of the largest growers, B. F. Tussing, got involved with the new community. He is credited with naming the village's north-south running streets after U.S. states. He is also credited with naming the village Fruitland as a way to attract attention to the area's orchards. When the railroad reached Fruitland in 1906, it immediately shipped apples from the John Bower packing house.

Because of the apple business, the tracks through Fruitland were lined by apple warehouses and packing plants. In 1931, these included F. H. Hogue (apple evaporator), Chaney & Rowell (apple warehouse and packing), F. H. Hogue (fruit warehouse, fruit and vegetable packing), Fruitland Fruit Association (packing), Fruitland Producers Association (vegetable warehouse), Henry Reins (apple warehouse and packing), and Palumbo-Arata Fruit (apple warehouse and packing). All of these were on the west side of the tracks, starting north of West 1st Street. The railroad had their depot on the west side of the tracks between SW 2nd and 3rd Streets.

None of these buildings still stand, but a few of the railroad tracks still exist. There is a 1900-foot siding to the west, where the packing houses once stood. There is also a 2400-foot-long siding near Milepost 6.0, where a spur track is used to serve Performix Nutrition Resources. In 1948, timetables show that there was a 14-car siding here, with a day operator in the depot using "FU" as its telegraph code. Trains #383 and #384 both stopped at Fruitland, scheduled for 7:30am and 2:25pm.

A post office opened in Fruitland in 1910. The community was incorporated as a village in 1948. Located 2225 feet above sea level in the Treasure Valley, Fruitland is today a town of about 5000 people, most of whom are involved with agriculture for a living. The area is the home of apples, onions, sugar beets, and the more famous Idaho Potato. Fruitland was named after the apple orchards that surround the community, and its slogan today is "The Big Apple of Idaho."

6.8  BUCKINGHAM – Coming in to Buckingham, the railroad crosses the Noble Canal and then turns to the east. This canal was one of the earliest built, constructed because a number of farmers weren't able to get the water they needed from the first canals. The Noble Canal, also known as the Noble Ditch, was built by John Bartsh to use the water rights of a Mr. Noble. By 1900, water was flowing.

Look for the Buckingham station sign at the Elmore Road grade crossing. Buckingham doesn't even make the *DeLorme Idaho Atlas & Gazetter* today, but in 1948, it was a typical siding which could hold 20 cars, pretty much a standard on rural Union Pacific branches in Idaho. In 1948, it was a 7:40am flag stop for mixed train #383, and 2:06pm for train #384. Today it is the Henggeler Packing facility (once the McMillan Fruit Company facility), located at 2244 feet above sea level.

Just east of Buckingham, the railroad again bridges over the Noble Canal. Union Pacific records showed this canal to be the Farmer's Canal.

**8.8    TOM THUMB** – In Union Pacific days, this was a small agricultural loading facility at 2233 feet above sea level. It has a 1200-foot siding to the north. In 2018, this was Archer-Daniels-Midland Company's Edible Bean Specialties facility.

The name Tom Thumb came about when the Idaho Canning Company was formed in 1903. The company used the *Seven Devils* label, and later the *Tom Thumb* label, for the dry beans and sweet corn that it canned. The company later became American Fine Foods.

Not far east of Tom Thumb, the railroad turns back to the southeast for a short distance.

*The Payette Branch*

IN&P #4506 heads east through Tom Thumb, passing between a recently harvested field of mint, and a field of corn that will soon be cut. This part of the railroad is heavily agricultural, with fields of sugar beets, potatoes, corn and alfalfa. Photo by Barton Jennings.

**11.1 NEW PLYMOUTH (NP)** – New Plymouth was a planned colony sponsored by The Plymouth Society of Chicago, a group from Chicago that was tired of city life. William E. Smythe, chairman of the executive committee of the National Irrigation Congress, was part of this group. Smythe was out to prove that irrigation in arid regions could create new towns and successful farms, and used the movement to attempt to prove his beliefs. The movement grew, and 250 families from the Midwest, and as far east as Boston, moved as a group to New Plymouth in 1895.

The name New Plymouth came about because Smythe felt that he was creating a new world, and named the town after the Plymouth Colony, reflecting the Boston influence and the ideals of the movement's founder. The town was platted with a horseshoe shape, with its open end facing to the north, toward the river. The area along the river was to be an industrial zone, and this is where the railroad built in 1906. The areas along the southern streets were to be residential.

The new residents each purchased 20 shares of stock at $30 per share, which gave them a town lot plus 20 acres of potential farmland. Each stockholder was also required to clear the land of sagebrush and plant fruit trees, preferably apples. A post office opened in 1896 soon after the community was incorporated on February 15, 1896. The community was named New Plymouth Farm Village, but became New Plymouth when it was incorporated as a village in 1908.

The community remained a small agriculture-based town for its entire history. City status was achieved in 1948. Today, New Plymouth is still a small agricultural community with a population less than 2000. In mid-August, New Plymouth hosts the Payette County Fair and Rodeo.

New Plymouth does have one major claim to fame today – it is the home of Truckstop.com. The firm was founded in 1995 by Scott Moscrip, considered by many as the first freight matching digital firm for freight shippers and motor carriers. The company provides load boards, mobile services, load tracking, and dozens of other services for both carriers and shippers. Truckstop.com will even help firms obtain their carrier and broker licenses. Today, the firm has the largest network of load boards, and is a leader in the transportation software field.

**The Payette Valley Railroad at New Plymouth**

In 1906, the Payette Valley Railroad built from Payette to New Plymouth to reach the growing apple and fruit business. Almost immediately, side tracks and fruit warehouses were built at the north end of town. According to a Sanborn Map Company map from August 1925, the siding to the north of the tracks at Ada Road (also known as West Boulevard) once served the New Plymouth Storage & Packing Company, and just to its east, the Payette Mills elevator. The railroad passenger station was on the south side of the tracks, with a baggage room on the west end, agent office in the middle, and waiting room on the east end. The station was at the end of Plymouth Avenue, one-half mile north of the New Plymouth post office. A siding looped around the south side of the station, serving the New Plymouth Growers Exchange warehouse, fruit packing and evaporator buildings, just to the southwest of the station. Union Pacific records also show that there were three stockyard pens here in 1930. Today, this area is simply a collection of small warehouses and assorted buildings.

New Plymouth was the end of the railroad from 1906 until the Payette Valley Extension Railroad built on to the east in 1910. When the railroad was extended, a track maintenance section was assigned to New Plymouth to work the track east of here. In 1948, mixed train #383 was scheduled to leave here at 8:00am, while westbound #384 came through at 1:55pm. There was a 33-car siding, and the railroad station had a day operator who used "NP" as its telegraph code. Coming into New Plymouth from Payette, the railroad turns back to the east at the edge of New Plymouth. All that is left of the series of tracks are a few short spur tracks on each side of the mainline.

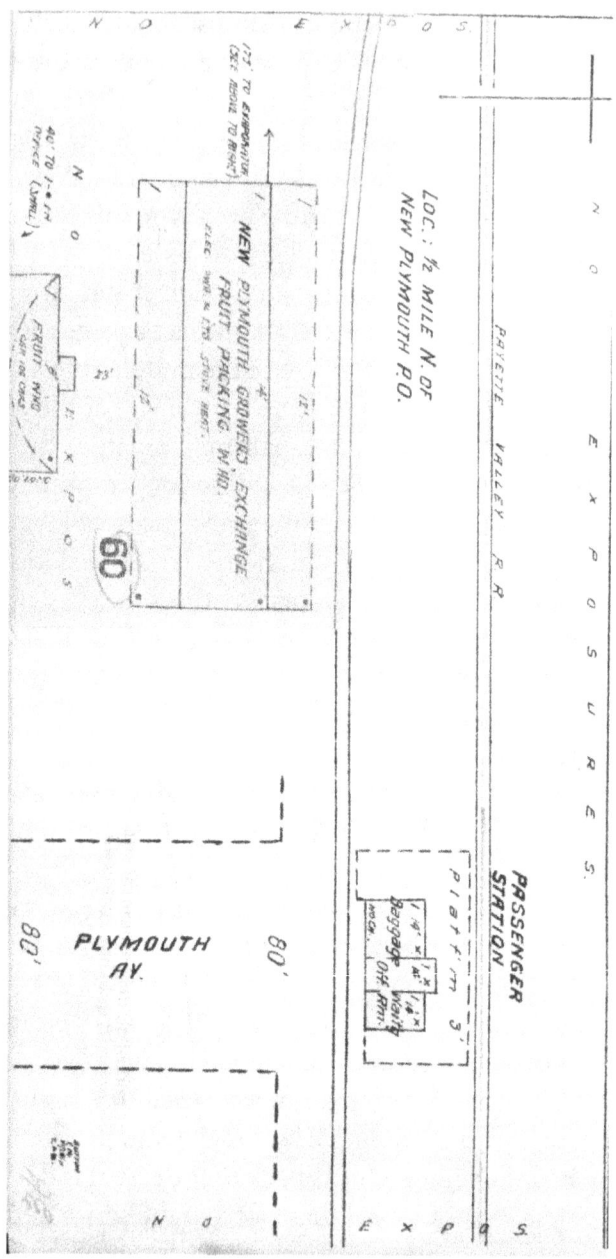

Sanborn Fire Insurance Map from New Plymouth, Payette County, Idaho. Sanborn Map Company, June - August 1925. Library of Congress. https://www.loc.gov/item/sanborn01646_002/.

**11.5** **DAVIS SPUR** – This retired side track is long gone. It was at an elevation of 2242 feet, and was located northeast of today's Payette County Fairgrounds. Heading east, the railroad crosses a number of the canals that make farming possible in the Payette River Valley.

**13.5** **IDAHO HIGHWAY 52** – Overhead is Highway 52, which stretches from Payette eastward to Emmett and on to Horseshoe Bend. The road basically follows the Payette River. The bridge that was built in 1936 was replaced in 2016.

The railroad curves to the southeast just east of this bridge. Heading toward Emmett, this is the longest tangent on the railroad. Between Mileposts 15.2 and 20.2, the track is straight. Nowhere else on the railroad is there anything close, with the 2.5-mile tangent stretch coming into Emmett being the next longest. Although the track is straight here, it is climbing a hill averaging about 0.2%.

**17.2** **FALKS** – Look for the grade crossing with Freemont Road. The community was to the north. Located on the Payette River, Falks was originally founded by David Bivens in 1862 when he built and began to operate a ferry across the river for the Boise-Payette road. Bivens sold the ferry to James Toombs in 1867, who soon opened a store to support his ferry. Nathan Falk acquired the operation a few years later and heavily promoted it in the area, resulting in the community taking Falk's name, often stated as Falk's Store or Falks Store. The bridge across the Payette River is known as the Falk Bridge.

In 1948, there was a five-car spur here. The mixed trains considered Falks as a flag stop. Train #383 passed at 8:16am while #384 passed at 1:34pm. There was also a freight platform for many years at Falks.

**17.6** **COUNTY LINE** – The county line is at the appropriately named County Line Road grade crossing. The county line runs north-south down the center of the road. To the west is **Payette County**, established on February 28, 1917, with its county seat at Payette. The county was once part of Canyon County. It was named for the Payette River, and is the smallest county in Idaho. The county has a population of about 25,000, and it is the home of the endangered Idaho ground squirrel.

To the east is **Gem County**, also a home to the Idaho ground squirrel, as well as less than 20,000 residents. Gem County, taking its name from the Idaho nickname, "Gem State," was established on March 15, 1915, from parts of Canyon and Boise counties. Emmett is the county seat and largest community in the county. Gem County is also relatively small, being the 40th largest of 44 counties in Idaho. However, at 560 square miles, it is more than half the size of the State of Rhode Island.

**18.9** **LITTLE ROCK** – This is another retired station that was built to serve the local agricultural industry. At one time, this was a busy nine-car, double-ended, loading track. Little Rock Road crosses the railroad where the track once was.

**20.8** **SEVEN MILE SLOUGH BRIDGE** – Look for the 13-span timber pile trestle. The railroad crosses this stream twice, here and to the east at Milepost 24.7, so it is clear that the slough is at least four miles long. However, according to several Idaho State sources,

## The Payette Branch

Sevenmile Slough (the way it is spelled in some documents) is fourteen miles in length.

**21.6 LETHA** – Letha is located on the north bank of Seven Mile Slough, not far south of the Payette River. The nearby fields have plenty of water for irrigation.

Letha was founded as part of the creation of the Payette Valley Extension Railroad. The founders of the railroad, W. W. Wilton and a Colonel Barnard, planned to develop a community half way between the ends of the railroad at New Plymouth and Emmett. On July 26, 1910, the plat for a town was filed using the name Letha, the only daughter of Wilton. Lots were sold by lottery on August 22, 1910, with the idea that the town would become a major rail center. Within a few years, Letha had a general store and a few other businesses. A small cheese factory was built on the corner of Cherry Street and Boise Avenue in 1912, but it didn't last very long. A post office in Letha also opened in 1912 (it closed in 1996). However, the expected growth never happened, and Letha is still an unincorporated community. The town provides some minimal support for area farms, including a small grocery store.

Although now gone, the railroad had a 13-car siding here in 1948, when eastbound train #383 could be flagged at 8:27am, and westbound #384 could be flagged at 1:23pm. There was also a single stockyard pen here, and a freight platform, in 1930.

**24.7 SEVEN MILE SLOUGH BRIDGE** – The railroad again crosses the stream, this time using a three-span steel pile trestle. One-half mile east of here, the railroad turns back to the east where it has a grade crossing with Cascade Road.

That is Vanderdasson Road immediately to the north. The Vanderdasson family moved to the Emmett area in 1887, ranching along the Payette River four miles west of Emmett.

**27.0 ENTERPRISE CANAL BRIDGE** – Construction on this canal system was started by the Enterprise Canal Company, but it failed before the project was completed. The Enterprise Irrigation District was formed to complete the project in 1905. The canal was officially completed on August 15, 1908. The canal is 22 miles long and waters more than 7000 acres of land.

The railroad crosses the Enterprise Canal on a three-span steel pile trestle. This location has also historically marked the western yard limits of Emmett. Yard limits is a form of authority to occupy a track. It requires any train to operate at a speed that allows them to stop in half the visible distance (restricted speed).

Not far to the east is a siding to the south that serves the Covia industrial silica sand facility. Silica sand is processed for glass and masonry products. The firm Covia was created in 2018 by the merger of Fairmount Santrol and the Unimin Corporation.

**28.5 BOISE PAYETTE LUMBER COMPANY** – To the north of the tracks are the foundations of what was once Weyerhaeuser's largest lumbering effort in Southern Idaho. On December 9, 1902, Weyerhaeuser chartered in Minnesota the Payette Lumber & Manufacturing Company. On December 24, 1913, the company was merged with the Baker Lumber Company, another Weyerhaeuser firm, to create the Boise Payette Lumber Company. Over the next several years, the firm acquired more timber in the region, and then opened a new sawmill at Emmett on May 10, 1917, rated at 400,000 board feet a day. Through 1923, the mill averaged producing 123 million board feet of lumber a year.

The mill at first relied upon logs floated down the Payette River, but timber losses were large. The company then supported the construction of a railroad along the river. Soon its entire supply was brought in by the railroad or truck. The mill was closed 1931-1933 due to the Depression, but operated near capacity during World War II producing Ponderosa pine lumber for many needs of national defense. However, there was already consolidation in the company as the Barber, Idaho, sawmill and box factory were closed and torn down in 1934. In 1957, Boise Payette Lumber and Cascade Lumber merged to create the Boise Cascade Corporation.

After several decades of change within Boise Cascade, the sawmill at Emmett closed in 2011 after 98 years of operation. After removing the mill, Boise Cascade gifted 34 acres of the mill site to the Idaho Foundation for Parks and Lands in 2017.

A railroad siding still exists and is used to hold cars awaiting delivery to shippers, usually the nearby Covia sand facility. A few other spur tracks into the mill site are also still in place, as are several buildings that are being promoted for other uses. This sawmill, and the Covia facility, explain why the Idaho Northern Branch track from Maddens to Emmett, and the track on the Payette Branch from Emmett west to Milepost 27.0, were leased to the Idaho Northern & Pacific in 1993 and not sold like most of the rest of the line.

The Boise Payette Lumber Company mill at Emmett cut lumber for the World War II effort. The lumber was used for ammunition cases, barracks, and other military uses. United States Office For Emergency Management. *Lumber manufacture. Building stockpiles for national defense. Ponderosa pine boards being stacked at the Emmet, Idaho sawmills of the Boise Payette Lumber Company. Efforts are being made to create a stockpile of lumber to insure a steady monthly output of ammunition cases. Lumber is also supplied from these mills for the construction of barracks and cantonments. Emmett. Gem County, Idaho, June 1941.* Library of Congress. https://www.loc.gov/item/2017690064/.

*The Payette Branch*

**29.1** **EMMETT JUNCTION** – This is the east end of the Payette Valley Extension Railroad, and then Union Pacific's Payette Branch. It is also the junction with the Idaho Northern Branch from Nampa, Idaho. While this was the end of the track built by the Payette Valley Extension Railroad, passenger trains operated to the downtown depot and freights ran to the nearby freight yards.

The milepost for the junction on the Idaho Northern Branch is 26.3. Once passenger trains stopped operating, the Payette Branch officially ended here.

**29.7** **EMMETT (MX)** – As stated, the downtown depot in Emmett was the end of the passenger route from Payette. Mixed train #383 was scheduled to arrive here at 8:50am, while train #384 was scheduled to depart back to Payette at 1:00pm.

For more information about Emmett please see page 79, where the route guide on up the Payette River continues.

*Idaho's Payette River Railroads: History Through the Miles*

# Idaho Northern Branch

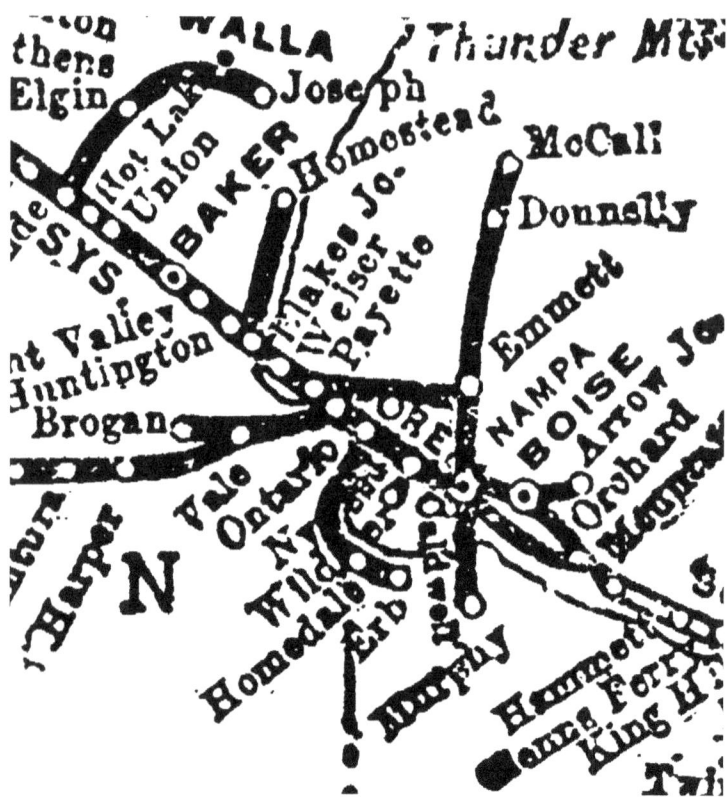

The *Official Guide of the Railways and Steam Navigation Lines of the United States Porto Rico Canada Mexico and Cuba,* February 1926, National Railway Publication Co., page 814, Map of the Union Pacific System.

## Idaho Northern Branch

Like the Payette Branch, the former Union Pacific Idaho Northern Branch was built in two efforts. The first 27 miles to Emmett were constructed in 1900-02 by the Idaho Northern Railway. The second construction push occurred 1911-1914 and extended the line from Emmett to McCall, Idaho. This latter effort started as an Idaho Northern Railway project, but finished under the control of the Oregon Short Line Railroad.

The line has been called one of the most spectacularly beautiful branch lines on the Union Pacific System. Both the Payette and the Idaho Northern Branches have traditionally been a part of Union Pacific's Idaho Division, part of the old Northwestern District. Union Pacific sold the Idaho Northern Branch to the Idaho Northern & Pacific (IN&P) as a part of a package of lines on November 15, 1993. While Union Pacific considered the line to be east–west, the Idaho Northern & Pacific considers it to be north–south, with Cascade to the north and Emmett to the south. Today, the Idaho Northern & Pacific route from Emmett to Banks is the Idaho Subdivision, while Banks to Cascade is the Cascade Subdivision.

**Idaho Northern Railway**

The Idaho Northern Railway was incorporated on December 17, 1897, but no construction took place for more than three years. Reportedly, construction on the Nampa to Emmett line began at Nampa on January 22, 1900. More than a year later on March 11, 1901, rail started to be laid, also at Nampa. The March 15, 1901, issue of *The Railway Age* stated that the line was being built by the Boise, Nampa & Owyhee, under the charter of the Idaho Northern Railway. It reported that 28 miles were graded and ready for the rails between Nampa and Emmett. The short article also stated that there was already a proposed extension of the line to Horseshoe Bend. At the time, J. M. Clark was operating as general superintendent and chief engineer of both railroads and showed his office as being in Nampa. Clark was involved with the railroad for a number of years and helped survey and design area roads and irrigation systems in addition to his railroad work.

*The Emmett Index*, dated April 3, 1902, reported that the first train arrived at Emmett on Saturday, March 29, 1902. In a typical article full of glowing statements and promises of future prosperity due to the railroad, the article carried the subtitle of "The Completion of the Enterprise Marks the Beginning of the Progress of Emmett and Surrounding Country." Some of the statements in the article showed even more flair, including "With the arrival of the railroad all realized that our bands of isolation are broken and now it is a fair field and no favors. Emmett has cause for congratulation. Her future was assured when the last spike of the Idaho Northern was driven."

If that wasn't enough, how about "Men of wealth have been long in taking advantage of our resources. It was not until Colonel Dewey, that broad minded and public-spirited citizen, conceived the project of a railroad to Emmett that we could hope for development of the country. It is ours now to demonstrate and verify the Colonel's faith in us. Let us work together for the advancement of Emmett and the Idaho Northern. The success of either means the success of both. The one is linked to the other by ties of interest. Long live Colonel Dewey, the Idaho Northern and Emmett, the garden spot of the valley."

Finally, concluding the article was the statement that "The month of March, 1902, is a red letter month for Emmett, and henceforth Emmett people will date events from the day the railroad came." While March 29, 1902, doesn't start the calendar for most in Emmett, it did begin a series of events that have impacted Emmett and the Payette River Valley ever since. Construction on the line between Nampa and Emmett was formally completed on April 30, 1902, and regular operations quickly began. The first timetable showed a daily Nampa to Emmett roundtrip, with train #1 departing Nampa at 3:00pm and arriving at Emmett at 4:30pm, only to depart back towards Nampa at 5:00pm as train #2, arriving at Nampa at 6:30pm.

**Colonel William H. Dewey**

The Colonel Dewey mentioned by the newspaper was Colonel William H. Dewey of Nampa. Dewey, who was born in Massachusetts in 1822 and headed to Idaho in 1863, was one of those people who seemed to have success with almost every venture he touched. Colonel Dewey was soon involved with building roads in Idaho, giving him access to information about the mines in the area. He helped create the new town that became Silver City, selected as the county seat of Owyhee County two years later. He also was a partner in the toll road that served the community. Dewey used his money to buy mines and mining properties, eventually owning nearly one-half of the South Mountain mines. Among his properties were the Trade Dollar and Black Jack mines, which he later sold to eastern companies.

Using the money he made selling off his mining interests, Dewey got involved with the railroad industry. His first project was the Boise, Nampa & Owyhee Railway, running toward his Owyhee mines, from Nampa to Murphy, Idaho. He also bought the dying town of Booneville, located northwest of his earlier Silver City. Dewey resurrected Booneville, which was soon renamed Dewey. The Idaho Northern Railway Company, Ltd. was his next venture. Dewey was the obvious head of the company as he owned 6940 of the 7000 shares. The railroad investment resulted in him also investing in Nampa, eventually owning 2000 lots in the city. To fill a few of the lots, he built the magnificent Dewey Palace Hotel. William Dewey died May 8, 1903, just a year after his hotel was built and the railroad opened to Emmett. His wife Belle managed his Nampa properties for many years, and part of downtown Nampa is now known as the Belle District in her honor.

Edward Henry Dewey, the oldest son of Colonel Dewey, took over for his father and ran many of the family businesses for several decades. The 1922 *American Elite and Sociologist Blue Book* called E. H. Dewey a farmer, stockgrower, banker and statesman. He held many titles such as president and owner of the Idaho Northern Railway Company; president and owner of the Dewey Electric and Power Company; president and owner of the Dewey Palace Hotel; president of the E. H. and W. C. Dewey Investment Company; president of the Idaho State Life Insurance Company of Boise; president of the Farmers and Merchants National Bank of Nampa; president of the Nampa Department Store; president of the Boise Valley Traction Company; and president of the Capital News Publishing Company of Boise. He was also a member of the Idaho State Senate, State Treasurer and State Mine Inspector.

**The Idaho Northern Railway Name**

One issue with the name Idaho Northern Railway was that there was also an Idaho Northern Railroad and a Pacific & Idaho Northern Railway. All eventually became part of Union Pacific. An article in the July 23, 1909, *Railroad*

*Age Gazette* highlighted an issue that this caused. The following article, entitled "A Change of Name Needed," is included here.

> The Idaho Northern Railroad Company runs from Enaville to Paragon, Shoshone County, Idaho, 33 miles. The Idaho Northern Railway Company operates between Murphy and Emmett, Idaho, 59 miles. At Nampa, 31 miles from Murphy, it connects with the Oregon Short Line. The first named company is in northern Idaho, having its general offices at Wallace, Idaho, on the Oregon Railroad & Navigation Company's line, while the second company is in southern Idaho, having its general offices at Nampa. Both roads are in the state of Idaho, but they are nearly 500 miles apart. Recently a ticket agent in Texas ticketing two old people destined for Emmett, which is in Southern Idaho on the line of the IN Railway, routed them by way of Denver, Billings, Wallace, and Enaville, and as a result, they were landed in Wallace without money and at least 500 miles from the point to which they had paid their fare.

## Idaho Northern Railway – Oregon Short Line

As the railroad was being built between Nampa and Emmett, there were plans to build a railroad up the Payette River. Even though the railroad was small, it was part of a large battle between E. H. Harriman's Union Pacific and James Hill's Northern Pacific. Each organization was trying to control the freight movements in the Northwest, leading them to buy up many of the smaller railroads and to build their own lines throughout the region. In 1910, Union Pacific acquired the controlling interest in the Idaho Northern Railway, with plans to reach the large timber holdings of Weyerhaeuser along the Payette River.

With the arrival of the Oregon Short Line-controlled Payette Valley Railroad at Emmett, the construction of a Payette River line again became a priority. In June 1911, construction began as a partnership between the Idaho Northern Railway Company Limited (controlled by the Dewey Syndicate) and the Oregon Short Line Railroad, using the resources of Union Pacific. The July 14, 1911, issue of the *Railway Age Gazette* announced that the Utah Construction Company had been awarded the contract to build "58 miles of grade from Emmett, Idaho, to Smith's Ferry." The Utah Construction Company later built the Western Pacific Railroad between Oakland and Salt Lake City, and then headed the formation of Six Companies to build the Hoover Dam. The August 11, 1911, issue added that there were four steel bridges and two important trestles, and that the line was being built to carry lumber, grain, hay, sheep and cattle.

The *Railway Age Gazette* (November 24, 1911) reported that grading work was under way on 56 miles of right-of-way, and that five miles of track had been laid. Details about the railroad's design was included, stating that much of the route passed through a rocky canyon, that there were four tunnels, and that the maximum grades were to be 2½ per cent. It was also reported that the line would be built "to a point about 103 miles from Emmett." All of the reports mentioned that E. H. Dewey was president and general manager of the railroad.

Grading had reached Banks by April 1912, and by August 1912, the track was completed between Emmett and Montour for a total of fourteen miles. This route included two short tunnels, but only got the railroad to the start of the Payette River Gorge. To simplify the construction contracts and clarify the railroad's ownership, the Idaho Northern Railway Company, and all of its properties, were sold to the Oregon Short Line Railroad Company on December 30, 1912. According to a June 30, 1907, report by the Interstate Commerce Commission, the Idaho Northern Railway owned 57 miles of track. This included the track owned by the Boise, Nampa & Owyhee Railway Company, which was sold to the Idaho Northern on January 21, 1907.

**Oregon Short Line Railroad**

After buying the railroad, the Idaho Northern Railway, including the Boise, Nampa & Owyhee Railway, was merged into the Oregon Short Line Railroad on January 6, 1913. By the time the Oregon Short Line fully acquired the Idaho Northern Railway, 2500 workers were involved in building the new line. Little changed in the contracts, and the railroad reached Smiths Ferry on July 10, 1913, and regular service began in late August. Reports indicate that all construction was completed between Nampa and Smiths Ferry by October 31, 1913. However, some other reports state that the railroad was completed to Smiths Ferry on October 29, 1912.

The July 17, 1913, issue of *Engineering News* had an article about the construction of the Emmett to McCall extension of the Idaho Northern line. It stated that grading began on July 1, 1911, and was completed on January 1, 1913, despite delays due to heavy snows during the winter of 1911-1912. The line was built with 75-pound ASCE (American Society of Civil Engineers) rail using railroad company forces. The first fifty miles was built using a Harris Track-Laying Machine, and then the rest of the line was built using a McCabe & Steen machine. The Harris Track-Laying Machine, originally designed by George Francis Harris in 1880, was a very popular track construction machine. The system used a "railroad on a railroad" system where rail carts on the machine moved supplies to the front of the machine. By 1887, one-fifth of all railway tracks in the United States were laid by the machine, according to *Appletons' Cyclopaedia of American Biography* (1901). The McCabe & Steen Track Laying Machine was a more modern version of the machine, built by the McCabe & Steen Construction Company. In August 1912, the McCabe & Steen Track Laying Machinery Company of Kansas City, Missouri, was incorporated to manufacture track laying machinery.

There were four steel truss spans and eight girder spans, equal to 900 feet in length. Additionally, there were 4000 feet of timber trestles and decking. The contractor also drilled four tunnels aggregating 844 feet in length. The fifth tunnel, which was to be 1166 feet in length, was cancelled due to a line change. About fifteen miles of the railroad grade used an old wagon road, and a new road grade was built further up the hillside. To move much of the material created by the blasting and digging, a 2-foot gage construction railroad using 12-pound rail was moved from location to location by the contractors.

The railroad was completed to Lakeport, today's McCall, on July 19, 1914, and over the next two decades, the Oregon Short Line Railroad operated the route as their Idaho Northern Branch.

**Union Pacific Railroad**

Union Pacific Railway created the Oregon Short Line Railway Company on April 14, 1881, a subsidiary designed to create the shortest rail route from Wyoming to Oregon. Both companies went through a bankruptcy during the late 1800s, with the result being Union Pacific Railroad controlling the Oregon Short Line Railroad (OSL).

During the early 1900s, Union Pacific (UP) Chairman Judge Lovett, who took control of the railroad after E. H. Harriman's death in 1909, proposed the consolidation of UP with its subsidiary roads. On May 10, 1932, UP stockholders approved the lease of the Oregon Short Line, plus several other subsidiaries and railroads. The consolidation proposal went to the Interstate Commerce Commission for approval almost immediately. At first, the proposal was denied on January 26, 1933, but was later approved on July 26, 1935, with a number of conditions, including the required acquisition of several other connecting companies.

On January 1, 1936, the Oregon Short Line was consolidated into Union Pacific. On that day, UP formally leased the railroad right-of-way and equipment of its subsidiaries, creating what was known as the Union Pacific System. Essentially, each subsidiary remained a company, its equipment, paychecks and other items still carrying their name, but Union Pacific operated all the railroads as one rail system. Because of bonding arrangements and other legal issues, many of these subsidiaries remained for more than fifty years. The railroad operated under the lease until December 30, 1987, when the OSL was fully merged into the Union Pacific Railroad.

On the Idaho Northern Branch, Union Pacific ran a daily except Sunday mixed freight and passenger train, plus extras when needed. The train often featured a few freight cars, numerous log cars bound for various sawmills along the route, and a coach and RPO/baggage car. Postal records show that from 1914 until 1948, there was a McCall & Nampa RPO (railway post office) on the "McCall Branch" of the Oregon Short Line, and later Union Pacific.

A unique part of the train was that it was one of the first to feature oil-fired steam locomotives on the Union Pacific System. This was due to several fires in 1941 which were blamed on embers from engines that burned coal. Because of weight restrictions on several bridges, the maximum class of steam locomotive on the Idaho Northern Branch was a Class 560 Consolidation (2-8-0). As many as three or four of these steam locomotives could be used on a single train, especially between Banks and Smiths Ferry where there were heavy grades. Diesel locomotives took over during the early 1950s.

In 1947, the track between Cascade and Donnelly was moved due to the construction of the Cascade Dam and Reservoir by the U. S. Bureau of Reclamation. In 1948, UP ran a northward mixed train #385 daily except Sunday, leaving Nampa at 8:30am and finally ending the day at McCall at 6:15pm after averaging 13.6 miles per hour. The train returned daily except Sunday as train #386, averaging 13.9 miles per hour. It departed McCall at 7:00am and arrived at Nampa at 4:30pm.

The trains became #485 and #486 by the January 1, 1950, public timetable, but still operated daily except Sunday. The passenger service was greatly sped up during the late 1950s, just in time for the line to lose its passenger service by the September 25, 1960, public timetable.

# Idaho Northern Branch
# Nampa to Maddens
## Union Pacific Idaho Northern Industrial Lead

The former Idaho Northern Branch still exists today between Nampa (Milepost 0.0) and north of Maddens (Milepost 7.0). It is currently operated as Union Pacific's Idaho Northern Industrial Lead. When most of the Idaho Northern Branch was sold to the Idaho Northern & Pacific (INPR) in 1993, Union Pacific kept ownership and exclusive operations of the first five miles of track to keep the Amalgamated Sugar Company business, as well as the business in several growing industrial parks near Nampa. Trackage rights were provided to the INPR between Nampa (Milepost 0.0) and near Maddens (Milepost 5.0) so they could interchange freight in the Nampa yard. Then, the line was leased to the INPR from Maddens to Emmett (Milepost 28.0). When the line between Maddens and Emmett was abandoned, Union Pacific kept these seven miles in service.

The telegraph code for each station, as shown in the *Union Pacific System List of Officers, Agencies, Stations, Etc. No. 60*, dated January 1, 1930, is included with the station name.

0.0 NAMPA (AU) – Nampa was originally a railroad town, created soon after the Oregon Short Line Railroad built a line through the area in 1883, connecting Granger, Wyoming, with Huntington, Oregon. In 1885, Alexander and Hannah Duffes homesteaded 160 acres in the area, and formed the Nampa

Land and Improvement Company in 1886 to create a townsite. Along with their partner James McGee, they began laying out a town. Their plan was for a religious community where no alcohol was available, and they refused to sell property to anyone planning on building a saloon. This quickly gave the town the nickname "New Jerusalem," although its official name was Nampa. However, the plan didn't work as by 1888, three of the 28 businesses in town were saloons. In fact, the Duffes' own house was moved in the early 1900s to make way for a new brewery.

Besides the railroad, the second major advancement at Nampa was water irrigation, which arrived in 1890 with the Phyllis Canal, and the Ridenbaugh Canal the next year. This opened several hundred thousand acres to farming. The Town of Nampa was incorporated on April 17, 1891. However, there is some uncertainty about the name Nampa. Many area railroad station names were believed to be of Indian origin. There is some evidence that supports the belief that Nampa could be a Shoshoni word meaning either moccasin or footprint.

About 1900, the next boom in the Nampa area came about when Colonel William H. Dewey, who made a fortune from mining in Silver City, started investing in the area. He built several railroads and the Dewey Palace Hotel. The hotel was completed in 1902 at a cost of a quarter of a million dollars. Dewey died the next year in his hotel and was buried in the Kohlerlawn Cemetery, leaving his son a million dollars.

In 1908, an annual harvest festival began that has become the Snake River Stampede Rodeo (first officially held in 1937). This event is still held annually and is rated as one of the top twelve rodeos in the pro rodeo circuits. 1926 saw the construction of a new Pacific Fruit Express refrigeration shop to support icing operations. A series of car shops were also erected to build and maintain refrigerator cars used for moving fruits and vegetables. These shops closed in 1982. Finally, the large Amalgamated Sugar mill was built in 1942, adding even more jobs to the area.

Nampa has been the home of Larry Jackson, Major League Baseball pitcher; Mark Lindsay, lead vocalist of the rock band *Paul Revere and the Raiders*; Rob Morris, former NFL linebacker for the Indianapolis Colts; and Ted Trueblood, editor of *Field & Stream* magazine.

Today, Nampa is the largest city in Canyon County, and the third largest city in Idaho. It has a population of slightly more than 80,000.

**Nampa Train Depot**

A major rail attraction in Nampa is the Nampa Train Depot, also known as the Oregon Short Line Depot. The building is listed on the National Register of Historic Places and houses the Canyon County Historical Society. Located at 12th Avenue and Front Street, this was actually the second of three passenger stations built at Nampa.

The first station was a small wooden building that was moved to Nampa from King Hill in 1887 to serve as a passenger depot. The need for a station came about because the Oregon Short Line (OSL) originally built south of Boise, and the Idaho Central Railway then built a line connecting Boise with the main line at Nampa. Reports are that the station was soon too small, especially after the Boise, Nampa & Owyhee and Idaho Northern railroads were built. Ticket sales alone reportedly exceeded $25,000 per month.

In 1900, the Oregon Short Line announced plans to build a new station at Nampa. The OSL, and its owner Union Pacific, announced plans to build "the finest depot on the line" at Nampa, at a cost of from $30,000 to $40,000. Frederick W. Clarke of Omaha, Nebraska, was the architect. Clarke designed a number of buildings in the Omaha area, including the Union Pacific Division Office and Commissary Building there in 1907.

The new depot building opened on September 25, 1903, measuring 113' 7" by 36' 10". The building was made from pressed brick and sandstone in a style the National Register describes as an "interesting eclectic combination of Romanesque, Renaissance, and Baroque elements, with the latter dominating. A massive central block of French Renaissance form is flanked by two advancing Baroque bays that bulge dramatically forward."

No matter the style, the new station was also soon too small, and in 1920, a new and larger station was built across the tracks to the north. This station was more than twice as big and had a baggage and express room on the east end, a waiting room and ticket office in the middle, and a news room with restrooms on each side on the west end. The older OSL station was immediately turned into office space for the railroad. For many years, the Assistant Superintendent of the Idaho Division was assigned to Nampa and used this building.

The Nampa Train Depot is a beautiful building that includes a number of unique architectural features found only in the stations that served larger cities along the line. Photos by Barton Jennings.

Nampa was always the origin and destination of the passenger trains operating on the Idaho Northern Branch. By 1948, both trains were mixed trains, operating daily except Sunday. Train #385 would leave Nampa at 8:30am, heading what was identified as westward to McCall, arriving there at a scheduled 6:15pm. Train #386 was scheduled to leave McCall at 7:00am and arrive at Nampa at 4:30pm. These trains often featured a coach and an RPO/baggage car, with thirty or more freight cars requiring as many as three steam locomotives. These train numbers dated from the 1920s.

Today, the "new" 1920 station has been converted into the Union Pacific office building and tower in Nampa. The original wooden station has been long gone. However, the OSL Depot from 1900 still remains, housing the Canyon County Historical Society, established in 1972 as a group designed to save the Nampa Train Depot from demolition.

Outside and to the east are several former Union Pacific items on display. The largest is former UP/OSL 902006, the last steam-powered derrick on Union Pacific. Retired in 1979, it had originally burned coal, but was changed to oil in July 1952. The derrick (a derrick on Union Pacific was used to clean up derailments) was built in June 1917 by Industrial Works, and was rated at 150 tons. With it is tender UP 907969 to supply water and oil to the derrick. This tender had earlier been with another derrick in Nampa. The third piece of equipment is UP caboose 3776. This was a Class CA-3 caboose built in June 1942. It was renumbered 25076 in February 1959, and retired in January 1980. All three items were donated to the Canyon County Museum during July 1988.

*Idaho Northern Branch – Nampa to Maddens*

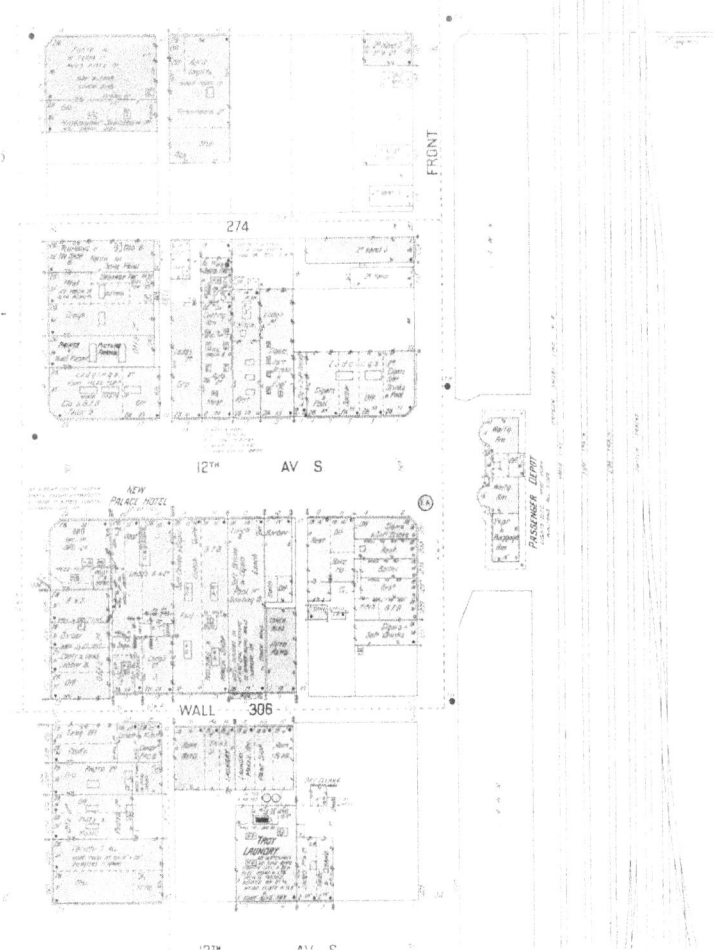

Sanborn Fire Insurance Map from Nampa, Canyon County, Idaho. Sanborn Map Company, Jan, 1921. Library of Congress, https://www.loc.gov/item/sanborn01644_006/.

### Union Pacific 616

Union Pacific 616, a 2-8-0, was donated to Nampa and is today displayed in Lakeview Park, several blocks to the north of the OSL Depot. This locomotive was assembled by the Baldwin Locomotive Works in July 1907, their Construction Number 31248. It was originally assigned to UP subsidiary Oregon Short Line Railroad as their #1066, and was renumbered to #616 in 1915. It became assigned to Union Pacific in 1936 and was donated to the City of Nampa in 1958.

**0.3** **IDAHO NORTHERN JUNCTION** – Located just west of 9th Avenue, this is the wye where the former Idaho Northern Branch turns north to head to Emmett. The former Oregon Short Line Boise Branch once broke off from the line just north of the wye, before being moved to the east end of the Nampa yard complex.

Near the west wye and south of the Union Pacific mainline and yard was the large Pacific Fruit Express (PFE) car repair shops complex. This is where the ice plant for the company once stood. Much of the PFE yard still exists and is used by the Boise Valley Railroad.

At the north wye switch, the railroad crosses over Indian Creek using a seven-span timber pile trestle. There are several industrial tracks and a siding in this area.

**1.0** **KOHLERLAWN CEMETERY** – The railroad passes through Kohlerlawn Cemetery, also known as the Nampa City Cemetery. On November 18, 1893, Dr. Fredrick S. Kohler, Nampa's first physician and surgeon, donated a parcel of land to Nampa to create a cemetery. A few years later, Mrs. Martha Weamer, an early Nampa settler, donated an additional two acres. Dr. Fredrick Kohler died in Nampa in 1908 and is buried in the cemetery that he helped found, and that is named after him.

Also buried here is Alexander Duffes, known as the founder of Nampa. Duffes was a railroad promoter and land developer who homesteaded 160 acres in Nampa, and later platted the town site of Nampa.

Colonel William H. Dewey, the backer of the Idaho Northern Railway, is also buried in Kohlerlawn Cemetery. Dewey built several railroads in the area, as well as the four-story Dewey Palace hotel, acclaimed as one of the finest in the West. Dewey is buried in Lot #286 to the west of the tracks, southeast of the intersection of Caba Avenue and Littleton Drive.

1.5   **INTERSTATE 84** – The railroad passes under Interstate 84, a 790-mile long highway from Portland, Oregon, eastward to Echo, Utah, east of Ogden. I-84 was once Interstate 80N, considered as a branch of Interstate 80. Built starting in the 1950s, it was renumbered in 1980.

2.6   **FISCHER** – To the west of the tracks is the reason why Union Pacific kept control of the lower part of the Idaho Northern Branch. This is the Amalgamated Sugar Company's Nampa facility. The company produces sugar in processing plants at Nampa, Paul, and Twin Falls, Idaho, as well as brown sugar at Nyssa, Oregon. The firm is based in Boise, Idaho, and processes sugar beets grown by the 750-plus members of the parent cooperative.

The firm dates back to 1897 when the Ogden Sugar Company was incorporated in Ogden, Utah. The Logan Sugar Company was formed in 1901, and the two merged in 1902 to create the Amalgamated Sugar Company, which quickly bought the Oregon Sugar Company. By 1918, the company had eight factories, with five in Utah and three in Idaho. It acquired the White Satin trademark in 1934, and began selling feed products for cattle and sheep in 1939.

In 1950, Amalgamated Sugar was listed on the New York Stock Exchange, but in 1997, the company was bought by the Snake River Sugar Company. This firm is known as the Cooperative and is owned by a number of sugar beet growers who sell their sugar beets to the company for processing.

The Nampa processing mill opened in 1942. Today, the three main mills (Nampa, Paul and Twin Falls) produce up to 1.6 billion pounds of sugar each year from 6 million tons of beets. The railroad hauls sugar, molasses, cattle feed and other products created or used by the mill. The Nampa mill produces the majority of the company's retail packaging, while the other mills handle more of the bulk customer shipments.

The name Fischer comes from John S. Fischer, who acquired a great deal of ranch and farm land in southern Idaho and eastern Oregon, some in this area. Today, the railroad has a four-track yard, plus several tracks into the sugar mill. The north end of the yard is at Milepost 3.0 at Cherry Lane. A Conrad & Bischoff rail-served petroleum tank farm is just north of Cherry Lane. The railroad now begins to pass through farm land, much of it growing sugar beets.

Train #385 was scheduled to be here at 8:40am and showed Fischer as a flag stop. However, train #386 had Fischer as a scheduled stop at 4:25pm. For many years, a unique feature of the Idaho Northern Branch was the Centralized Traffic Control signal system on the first 2.4 miles between Nampa and Fischer.

**4.0** **YARD LIMITS** – Because of the switching required at the Amalgamated Sugar mill, southbound trains were required to operate at restricted speed – the ability to stop in less than half the sight distance – from here to Nampa. This location is at the Ustick Road grade crossing.

When the railroad was first built, there was a station here known as Leonard or Leonards.

**6.0** **MADDENS** – While the timetable for the Idaho Northern Industrial Lead shows Maddens at Milepost 4.8, it has historically been several short sidings to the west at Milepost 6.0, near the grade crossing with U.S. Highway 20. Train #385 could be stopped by flagging at 8:50am, while train #386 could be flagged at 4:15pm.

Today, Sunroc (asphalt and concrete paving and construction) is the major customer here, although the foundations of older customers can still be found. While this area is still mainly agricultural, a number of new suburbs from nearby Caldwell are being developed close to the west.

**6.8** **OREGON TRAIL** – Union Pacific track profiles traditionally included historic landmarks. This location was noted as being a crossing of the Oregon Trail. This trail was almost 2200 miles long, running from near Independence, Missouri, to the Willamette Valley in Oregon, and even up into Washington State.

The trail was used from the early 1830s until the 1870s and later, however its peak years were 1846-1869. During this time, migrant wagon trains were used by more than 400,000 people to reach what was considered by many to be a utopia.

**7.0** **END OF TRACK** – The end of the track is north of the siding at Sunroc. The track north of here was officially abandoned on February 29, 1996.

# Idaho Northern Branch
## Maddens to Emmett
### Abandoned

From Milepost 7.0, north of Maddens, to Milepost 24.5, south of Emmett, the railroad has been abandoned. This part of the line was never a major revenue source. Instead, it was used to move freight to and from the Payette River Valley area. As the volumes of freight dropped, so did the benefit of the line, especially when the much flatter Payette Branch was available.

In late 1993, the Idaho Northern & Pacific leased the line for operations from Milepost 5.0 near Maddens, to Milepost 28.0 near Emmett. The company also bought the Payette Branch, meaning that only that freight that needed to go to or from the Nampa area would use this route. Within several years, the railroad determined that freight could be interchanged at Payette just as easily and at a lower cost. With the Idaho Northern & Pacific pulling their business from the route, Union Pacific applied to abandon the line on December 6, 1995. With quick approval, the abandonment took effect on February 29, 1996.

A report on the abandonment hearings by the State of Idaho had some very interesting information. It stated:

> The hearing examiner also found, that when Idaho Northern leased this trackage from Union Pacific, it originally used one locomotive to take cargo over this branch. However, because the Freeze-Out Hill near Emmett was so steep Idaho Northern added

> *additional locomotives as the number of rail cars increased. The additional locomotives coupled with the larger trains caused a fire on the Freeze-Out Hill area in 1994. Idaho Northern received a bill from the Bureau of Land Management for $68,000 as the result of this fire. Therefore, he concluded, that using additional locomotives are more expensive, causes more wear and tear on the tracks and requires more maintenance. Idaho Northern indicated that it would use the alternative route of the Payette Valley line to avoid the danger of igniting fires from the locomotives.*

Because the railroad has been abandoned for only several decades, the grade is generally still easy to find and follow. However, especially where the line once passed through farm land, parts have been completely removed to gain more acreage for planting. In other areas, official and unofficial trails use the grade.

Each station along this route is described, and in many cases, a description of where its remains can be found is provided. The telegraph code for each station, as shown in the *Union Pacific System List of Officers, Agencies, Stations, Etc. No. 60*, dated January 1, 1930, is included with the station name.

7.0 **END OF TRACK** – The end of the track is north of the siding at Sunroc. The track north of here was officially abandoned on February 29, 1996. Not far north of here are a number of gravel and sand pits, many operated by Idaho Materials and Construction.

8.4 **BOISE RIVER BRIDGE** – This bridge crossed the southern channel of the Boise River, which for much of the year simply serves as an overflow channel. The railroad used a five-span steel pile trestle.

8.5 **BOISE RIVER BRIDGE** – This was the railroad bridge over the primary channel of the Boise River. From south to north, the bridge consisted of ten timber pile spans, and then six through plate girder spans, each 62 feet long. Built as a replacement structure in 1916, the bridge still stands next to the Middleton Road bridge.

The Boise River was originally known as Reed's River for John Reed, an employee of the Pacific Fur Company. Reed is credited with exploring the river in 1813 and 1814. The river forms from three separate branches that all start in the Sawtooth Range in southwestern Idaho, northeast of Boise. The river is approximately 100 miles long, ending as it flows into the Snake River three miles south of Nyssa, Oregon.

The river is dammed in several places and is used as a water source for a number of irrigation canals. Many of the facilities were built as part of the Bureau of Reclamation's "Boise Project." This campaign began in 1905 to provide irrigation water for the sagebrush valleys, and drinking water for the developing communities. The project included the construction of five major reservoirs, two principal diversion dams, three sizable pumping plants, three power plants, and a number of related facilities.

North of this bridge, the right-of-way has been paved and is used as a walking and biking trail, and is known as the Middleton Bike Trail. It runs from here northward to near downtown Middleton.

**8.7  GRAVEL SPUR** – The railroad once passed through a large series of mining pits, used for construction gravel. This one was located to the west and has since been reclaimed.

**9.6  MIDDLETON (KD)** – Middleton is considered to be the oldest settlement in Canyon County. In 1863, William N. Montgomery acquired land here. Located on the Boise River, it quickly became an important location. It became a common rest stop for travelers moving between the old Fort Boise and Keeney's Ferry, both well-known wagon train stops. Middleton was named for its location between Boise and Keeney's Ferry, and it served as a stop during the early days of the Oregon Trail. It obtained a post office in 1866, and a grist mill opened on the river in 1871. Its population in 1870 was 44 residents.

The future of Middleton became uncertain when the Boise River flooded in 1872 and cut a new channel around Middleton, putting it on an island. By 1880, the town had moved back north of the river. Middleton was incorporated in 1910, but the paperwork wasn't completed until 1971. Today, Middleton's population is approximately 6000, and its motto is "Life is Better Here."

Located at an elevation of 2401 feet, the railroad once had several spur tracks to the west, plus a single stockyard pen. Much of the railroad's route through downtown has been changed, so little still exists to indicate that a railroad once passed through town. However, the main north-south road in downtown Middleton is Dewey Road (Milepost 9.5), a tribute to the builder of the railroad. In 1948, Middleton had a 14-car siding, and train #385 made a stop here at 9:00am, while #386 was here at 4:05pm.

In 1930, Middleton was the home of Section Gang #491, which maintained the track between Nampa and Jenness. Heading north, the railroad grade is becoming lined with new housing subdivisions, an indication of the growth that the region is experiencing. For a short stretch, the new Wanda Way road uses the grade about Milepost 10.5.

**Boise Valley Traction Company**

Just west of the Idaho Northern Railway grade at Cornell Street is the former Boise Valley Traction Company Middleton Substation. The substation was actually built by the Idaho Traction Company in 1912 as a part of an upgrade of what was called the Boise Valley Loop, a 70-mile interurban railway loop around the region.

The 16' x 30' Italianate-style building was listed on the National Register of Historic Places in 1973. The building originally featured an office and a transformer room, and has a two-story tower centrally located over the front entrance. The exterior was covered with stucco, and the roof was once covered with cedar shingles. The building was later used as a small civic center and meeting room. In 2015, the building was restored and turned into the Lee Moberly Museum, named for the former Middleton postmaster and local historian.

Next to the substation, a brick power station was built to supply electricity to the interurban system. It also powered the first electric lighting for Middleton. The museum has since expanded the transformer building to connect it to the adjacent structure.

The Boise Valley Loop and the Boise Valley Traction Company had the typical history of several competing companies eventually falling under the control of one larger company. The Boise Valley Loop started in Boise and went west to Nampa, and then northwest to Caldwell. From there, the route turned to the northeast to Middleton, and then east and southeast back to Boise, creating a large loop around the valley.

Construction began in 1905, and on August 8, 1907, the northern part of the Loop was finished by the Boise Interurban Railway from Boise to Middleton and on to Caldwell, with full service beginning on August 16th. The southern part of the Loop had a more complex history. In 1906, the Boise Valley Railway Company built a curvy route from Boise to Meridian. By 1910, this line had been extended to Nampa. In 1911, the Boise Valley Railway Company was sold to the Kessel-Kinnicut Company, which extended the line on to Caldwell, and then built an improved Boise-Nampa line in 1912, just in time for service to open to Caldwell on June 6, 1912.

Soon after, both the north and south sides of the Loop were merged into the Idaho Railway, Light and Power Company, which operated the line through its Idaho Traction Company subsidiary. By 1913, the Idaho Railway, Light and Power Company had entered receivership. The result was that by 1915, the Boise Valley Traction Company, owned by the Idaho Power Company, owned and operated the interurban railroad.

The railroad remained profitable until 1920, and as passengers began to buy their own cars, freight took on more importance. While some of this freight was small package deliveries, most was agricultural products like sugar beets. An article in the *Electric Railway Journal* (October 13, 1923) stated that the railroad "extends from Boise along the north bank of the Boise River to Middleton. There it connects with the Oregon Short Line Railroad's Idaho Northern branch. It then crosses the river and connects with the main line of the Oregon Short Line at Meridian." The Boise Valley Traction Company interchanged freight at both junctions, using freight cars supplied by the Oregon Short Line. This wasn't enough to cover the costs of operating the railroad, and on May 17, 1928, all operations ceased.

12.4 **JOSEPHSON** – This station was located where the railroad crossed Gallaway Road, once known as Douglas Lane. There was a 550-foot-long siding here in 1976. In this area, the old grade is used as driveways to several new homes. Heading north, trains faced a 1.0% grade, going from 2456 feet at Josephson to 2537 feet near Milepost 14.2. This was required to get out of the East Hartley Gulch.

13.5 **AMSCO** – Amsco, a 550-foot-long siding, was located just south of the grade crossing with Goodson Road, once known as Elm Lane. In 1939, the land was shown to be the property of the United States government. Heading north, the railroad grade crosses Spur Line Road and then follows Emmett Road, which is to the west of the grade. The climb to Jenness starts at Milepost 15.0, and follows West Hartley Gulch, and then Little Freezeout Canyon.

16.8 **COUNTY LINE** – There is little to mark the county line on the railroad grade, but signs on Little Freeze Out Road do mark the location. The name of the road also changes, from Emmett Road in Canyon County, to Little Freeze Out Road in Gem County.

To the south is **Canyon County**, created on March 7, 1891, and organized on November 26, 1892, with the election of various government positions. The county was once much larger, but some land was spun off as Gem County was formed in 1915, and then Payette County in 1917. The name Canyon County comes from the canyons in the area, although there is argument whether it was the Snake River canyon or the Boise River canyon near Caldwell. The county seat is Caldwell, while the largest city in the county is Nampa. The county's population in the 2010 census was 188,923, making it the second-most populated county in Idaho.

To the north is Gem County. **Gem County** is noted as being a home to the rare Idaho ground squirrel, as well as less than 20,000 residents. Gem County, taking its name from the Idaho nickname, "Gem State," was established on March 15, 1915, from parts of Canyon and Boise counties. Emmett is the county seat and largest community in the county.

18.8 JENNESS – Jenness was at the top of the grade at 2651 feet in elevation. It was known as Summit in 1906. There was a short 715-foot-long siding to the east. From the south, the grades reached 1.0%. Trains coming south faced grades of 2.05%.

For those who are interested, the Jenness series of soils are found in southwestern Idaho, and consist of very deep, well drained soils on bottomlands, low terraces, and alluvial fans. They formed in alluvium and colluvium from acid igneous rocks. The soils are used for rangeland and irrigated cropland. Small grains, corn, sugar beets, alfalfa, and improved pasture are grown on irrigated land. Vegetation in the potential natural plant community is sagebrush, bluebunch wheatgrass, Sandberg bluegrass, Thurber needlegrass, and giant wildrye.

Jenness, shown as Jenness Hill in some documents, was a flag stop for both trains. This was likely due to the need for trains to stop to test brakes before going down the steep grades. Train #385 was scheduled to be here at 9:20am while #386 was to be here at 3:40pm.

The name Jenness is unique. Ned Jenness bought the *Leader Herald* of Nampa in 1907, one of several newspapers he owned and edited. He also served as postmaster in Nampa, and as president of the Commercial Club, later the Nampa Chamber of Commerce. Jenness made a number of investments in land in southwest Idaho. The name of Summit was changed to honor Ned Jenness.

Heading north, the railroad begins a series of sharp curves and loops as it descends into the Emmett Valley. The grade is often clearly visible from Little Freeze Out (or sometimes Freezeout) Road.

**Freezeout Hill**

The grade from Bramwell to Jenness received the name Freezeout Hill, taken from that used for a nearby wagon road. Several attempts had been made to build a road down off of the hill to the south of Emmett, but the steep, sheer drop was too much. However, in 1862, Tim Goodale opened an Oregon Trail Cutoff which descended a steep ridge, providing a curvy route into the Emmett Valley. The road was so steep that wagons often had to have their wheels locked so they slid down the hill to keep them from running away. Wagons going up the hill often required as many as twelve horses and a good part of a full day to make the climb.

The name Freezeout (also spelled Freeze Out and Freeze-Out) has two origins, according to different sources. One is that to freeze a wagon's axle meant to lock it up so it couldn't roll, the process used going down the hill. Another version comes from a story about surviving the hill during a winter storm, a version told on several historical markers in the area.

> In the winter of 1864 a freighter and another wagon of valley residents came upon the grade. The weather was bitter with freezing rains, snow and wind. The frozen earth made it impossible to descend. They attempted to rough-lock and lower their wagon, but it slid out of control and into a gulch. They returned to the top and camped with the freighter. Upon reaching home many told the story with the words, "We likely froze to death. We were froze out of the valley."

**20.7 BLACK CANYON CANAL BRIDGE** – This is a major irrigation canal that takes water from the lake created by Black Canyon Dam on the Payette River, and provides irrigation water to approximate 53,200 acres that are part of the Black Canyon Irrigation District, plus 5100 acres for the Emmett Irrigation District. Black Canyon Dam is about five miles northeast of Emmett, and was completed in 1924. Construction on the canal began in 1936, and was finished by 1940. The project was built by the Bureau of Reclamation, and managed by them until January

1, 1955. Responsibility for the operation was then given to the Black Canyon Irrigation District.

The railroad crossed the canal using two 50-foot deck plate girder spans. The bridge spans are still in place. Heading north, the grade is used as a road to follow the canal to the east, which uses a tunnel (Tunnel #7) to pass through the nearby hill.

**21.1** **SAND** – This long-retired station was near where the rail grade approaches today's South Slope Road. In 1932, there was a 642-foot siding here.

**22.1** **BRAMWELL** – Bramwell is an unincorporated community in Gem County, located at an elevation of 2375 feet. The community started in 1902, not long after the railroad was built. It was named after Franklin S. Bramwell, a Mormon leader. Franklin had served a number of tasks for the church and was honored by having a small church branch named for him in this area. The town used the church name.

Bramwell was never a large place, and was a flag stop for the railroad, with #385 at 9:35am and #386 at 3:25pm. Heading toward Emmett, the railroad turned straight east through the community and crossed the Farmer's Cooperative Canal at Milepost 22.2. The seven-span timber pile trestle was removed after the railroad closed. The Farmer's Cooperative Canal takes water from the Payette River, northeast of Emmett, flows through town, and then south to here. It flows west to serve the farms below those that rely upon the Black Canyon Canal.

Trains heading toward Nampa often used Bramwell to double Freezeout Hill. The rear half, including the passenger cars, would be left here while the front half of the train was taken to the top of the grade at Jenness. The locomotive would return and then take the second half to the top of the hill, reassemble the train, and then head to Nampa. This would give passengers plenty of time to wander the small settlement.

The right-of-way north of this canal and to the northeast is used as some local farm roads, crossing several more irrigation canals. Just north of Bramwell is the bottom of the 2.05% grade up to Jenness. The elevation is 2332 feet, more than 300 feet lower than the top of the hill just a few miles away.

24.0  YARD LIMITS – This was the yard limits for northbound trains approaching Emmett. It was just north of Sale Yard Road (Milepost 23.75).

To the east is the northwest end of the City of Emmett Municipal Airport – Chuck Sawyer Field. The field was an Army Air Corps civilian pilot training facility during World War II. It was named to honor Colonel Chuck Sawyer, a member of the Flying Tigers. Credited with two air-to-air kills, he was forced down near Tibet and made a 200-mile trek on foot to evade captors. He later became one of five members who joined the United States Army Air Force 23rd Fighter Group.

24.5  END OF TRACK – The track from Emmett ends just north of the end of Runway 10 of the City of Emmett Municipal Airport. The Gem County Golf Course, a nine-hole course, surrounds the airport.

# Idaho Northern Branch
# Emmett to Cascade
## Idaho Northern & Pacific

The former Idaho Northern Railway line, later the Idaho Northern Branch of Union Pacific, was turned over to the Idaho Northern & Pacific (INPR) in late 1993. As already noted, the trackage was used by the INPR under three different methods: sale, lease, and trackage rights. The track from the end of the abandonment at Milepost 24.5 to Milepost 28.0, just east of Emmett, was at first leased to the INPR. From Milepost 28.0 to Cascade, the Idaho Northern & Pacific bought the line.

During the 1940s, trains heading from Nampa to Emmett and on to Cascade and McCall were considered to be running westward by the railroad. This definition of direction continued until the mid-1980s when the line was changed to north-south, with trains heading north to Cascade being northbounds, and trains heading to Nampa southbounds. The Idaho Northern & Pacific has continued the use of these directions.

However, there have been some other changes. Under Union Pacific, the Idaho Northern Branch went all the way from Nampa to McCall, a total of 132.8 miles. Trains #385 and #386 served the entire route, each making a one-way trip over the line daily except Sunday. With the abandonment of the line north of Cascade, the route became shorter. However, the INPR broke the line up into even shorter sections, with the **Idaho Subdivision** running from Emmett to Banks, and the **Cascade Subdivision** running from Banks to Cascade.

The following route guide covers the Idaho Northern Branch from Emmett to Cascade. The telegraph code for each station, as shown in the *Union Pacific System List of Officers, Agencies, Stations, Etc. No. 60*, dated January 1, 1930, is included with the station name.

**24.5   END OF TRACK** – The end of the track from Emmett is just north of the end of Runway 10 of the City of Emmett Municipal Airport. The Gem County Golf Course, a nine-hole course, surrounds the airport. The Idaho Northern & Pacific wound up owning the few miles of track in this area that they previously leased (Mileposts 24.5 to 28.0).

Early reports about the construction of the line across the valley area indicate that this was swampy land. In many places, pine pilings had to be installed as part of the track work to stabilize the railroad grade.

**25.1   IDAHO HIGHWAY 52** – This is a grade crossing with Highway 52, which stretches from Payette eastward to Emmett and on to Horseshoe Bend. The road basically follows the Payette River. There are several tracks that once served, or currently do serve, rail shippers. To the south of the highway is a siding to the west that once served "Cold House." A few foundations and a small warehouse remain. North of the grade crossing is a spur track to the east into an Ed Staub & Sons propane storage and distribution facility.

**26.0   EMMETT YARD** – Located between Tyler Road (25.7) and Cascade Road (26.3) is a small two-track yard to the west of the old mainline. This yard allows the railroad to switch and store rail cars outside of the Emmett downtown area.

**26.3  EMMETT JUNCTION** – This is the junction with the Payette Branch. The milepost for the junction on the Payette Branch is 29.1. When passenger trains operated, both lines shared the track to the train station in Emmett, and both mileposts were used to there. Later, the Payette Branch officially ended here.

**26.9  EMMETT (MX)** – It can be said that Emmett came about initially because some people heading to Oregon on the Oregon Trail didn't make it all the way. By the 1850s, wagon trains headed to Oregon were passing through the rich valley, and some homesteads began to be settled. In 1864, a ferry opened across the Payette River known as Martin's Ferry. Nathaniel Martin and Jonathan Smith had opened a roadhouse on the river that year, working to attract the business of the wagon trains. The community grew, using the name Martinsville.

A competing community seven miles to the west obtained a post office in 1870. Thomas Cahalan was the first postmaster, and he named the post office Emmettville after his son Emmett. In 1876, the post office was moved to the larger Martinsville, and the name came with it. In 1883, James Wardwell had the town platted and lots began to be sold. The name of the town and post office was shortened to Emmett in 1885. Emmett was officially incorporated in 1900.

The arrival of the railroad and irrigation allowed the region to open up for commercial farming and ranching. Soon, fruits and vegetables, cattle and sheep, lumber, and ice production started to bring wealth to the community. The railroad built their own five-pen stockyards to handle the livestock shipments. Movements were so large that Emmett became the largest Idaho shipping center on the Union Pacific during the late 1920s.

During the past decade or two, Emmett has had to survive several pieces of bad news. The worst of these was the closing of the large Boise Cascade sawmill. However, Emmett is the county seat of Gem County, and the county's only city. Its population has continued to grow slowly, with 6557 residents in the 2010 census. The city sits in the middle of Emmett Valley at an elevation of 2373 feet, surrounded by mountains.

Across Washington Avenue, east of the Emmett Depot, is the **Martin-McNish Parking Lot**, named for two important people in Emmett's history. The Martin part honors Nathaniel Martin, founder of Martinsville, now Emmett. The name McNish honors John McNish, who carried a number of titles during the developing days of Emmett. McNish started a local sawmill that was bought by Boise Payette Lumber in 1917. He was also a teacher, a city trustee, vice president of the First National Bank, promoter of irrigation canals, and partner in a general merchandise store. McNish was a major proponent of the creation of Gem County and served as chairman of the first commissioners of the county. Basically, there was little in the area that he didn't support or get involved with.

## The Railroad at Emmett

Emmett was a junction town, connecting the Payette Branch and the Idaho Northern Branch, both owned and operated by Union Pacific. The Idaho Northern Railway arrived here by 1902, and the Payette Valley Extension Railroad arrived in 1910. It wasn't until 1911 that construction started east up the Payette River. By this time, the Oregon Short Line, a part of Union Pacific, had already started to centralize their facilities, and Emmett received just enough investments to do their job. Therefore, Emmett never developed a large list of railroad facilities. However, its 50,000-gallon water tank had a spout that was shown as an obstruction during the 1930s. The water was supplied from a nearby well that was east of the station.

The local rail business focused primarily on lumber and agricultural crops. The 1920s were good years for the railroad at Emmett. According to the National Register of Historic Places, car shipments from Emmett in 1924 "included 2,332 cars of forest product, 433 of fruit, 23 of wool, 10 of lettuce, 96 of livestock, 29 of grain and 105 of miscellaneous freight. The 1923, fruit shipments were 1,265 cars with 1924 being a poor year for fruit." Information for 1928 shows that Emmett "had become the largest shipping point in Idaho on the Union Pacific Railroad lines." Volumes for that year were a total of 4300 boxcar loads originated at Emmett, "including: 2,400 of lumber, 540 of apples, 200 of prunes, and 100 of livestock."

During the 1920s, the Boise Payette Lumber Company (later Boise Cascade), located on the west side of town. It was a heavy shipper of lumber, and receiver of timber and rough lumber. Just to the mill's east was a wye track that was used for turning locomotives, and to serve an industrial track on the south bank of the Payette River along Barton Street. This wye track still exists. The Cloud-Field Company pea cannery once stood to the south of the wye.

Maps from the Sanborn Map Company show that a spur track ran along the north side of the irrigation canal that flows through town. This track served packing houses of several fruit shippers, including the Earle Fruit Company of the Northwest, and the Fruit Growers Union. Some of these buildings still survive on Canal Street. East of the depot and south of the irrigation canal, other shippers such as Denney & Company (several fruit warehouses), an eight-bin coal shed, and Emmett Fruit Growers stood along several sidings.

The railroad had a small yard at the east end of town, plus a siding shown to be 4510 feet long. Most of these tracks still remain today. In 1930, the railroad used a freight car scale located at the Boise Payette Lumber Company. There was also a track maintenance section based here that maintained the track between Jenness and Milepost 35.3. Today, Emmett is the headquarters of the Idaho Northern & Pacific, located in the old wooden depot, built in 1924. Locomotives and other equipment of the railroad can generally be found here.

*Idaho Northern Branch – Emmett to Cascade*

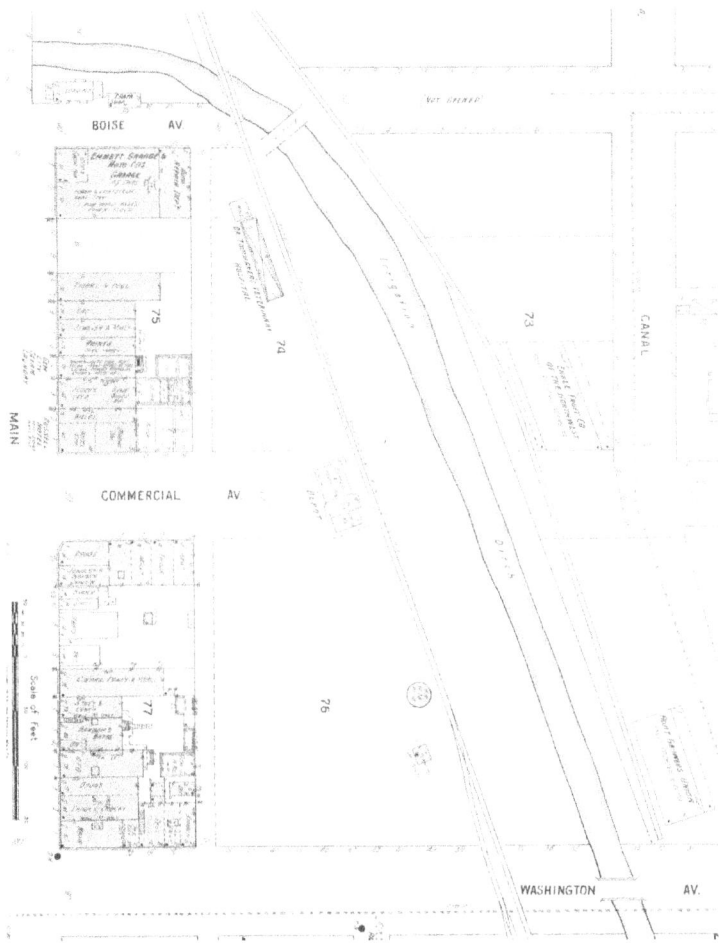

Sanborn Fire Insurance Map from Emmett, Gem County, Idaho. Sanborn Map Company, November 1917. Library of Congress, https://www.loc.gov/item/sanborn01594_003/.

Even into the 21st Century, there were still many signs of the old days along the railroad. Here in Emmett, there was a wooden boxcar that had been turned into a yard office and tool shed, still standing in August 2003. Photo by Barton Jennings.

## The Oregon Short Line Railroad Depot

The depot building that stands alongside the tracks at the north end of Commercial Avenue is not the original depot at Emmett. The original depot was built at the same location soon after the railroad arrived in 1902. The structure featured an express and freight room at the west end, a ticket office in the center, and a waiting room on the east end.

The current depot was built in 1924 by the Oregon Short Line Railroad, owned by Union Pacific. This new depot isn't actually all new, as the freight room on the east end was actually reused from the earlier structure. It was moved to the east end and connected with the new depot under one roof. This redesign made the new depot much larger than the old station, measuring approximately 108'-0" x 26'-6". From west to east, the new station featured a pair of restrooms and lounges, a waiting room, a ticket office, an express baggage room, and a freight room.

As was common, the 36'-6" x 24'-6" freight room is raised four feet to match the doors of freight cars and motor vehicles.

In 1948, mixed train #383 from Payette arrived here at 8:50am and passengers going on toward Cascade and McCall would sit around the depot until mixed train #385 would arrive from Nampa shortly before 10:00am. After some switching, #385 would depart northward at 10:20am. Heading in the other direction, train #384 departed at 1:00pm for Payette. This did not allow for a connection with the train from McCall (#386), as it was scheduled to get here before 3:00pm, do some freight work, and then depart at 3:10pm.

During the 1940s, Emmett had a daytime operator in the station, using the telegraph code "MF" instead of the earlier "MX." The operator and register book was active at Emmett through the 1970s.

The depot remained open and in use until 1964. Over the past few decades, the building has been used for storage and other purposes, and some changes in its design have taken place. For example, the Union Pacific seals that were once located beneath the entrance hoods have been removed. Additionally, exterior doors have been added to the restrooms, the restrooms have been combined, and the interior floor plan has been changed. Finally, the track-side platform on the north side is now gone.

The depot is listed on the National Register of Historic Places and is used as offices by the Idaho Northern & Pacific. Another feature of the depot area is the traditional depot grounds park. Located across the street to the southeast is Blaser Park, the home of the Emmett Farmer's Market. An early name for the park was Blaser Railroad Park.

*Idaho's Payette River Railroads: History Through the Miles*

The Emmett depot still stands and is now used as the offices of the Idaho Northern & Pacific Railroad. Photo by Barton Jennings.

The Emmett depot features the freight section on the east end (now railroad-north), as shown here in 2003. Photo by Barton Jennings.

**28.7 LAST CHANCE CANAL BRIDGE** – The canal is crossed by the railroad using a single span timber bridge. During the 1890s, area settlers created the Last Chance Canal Company to create a system of irrigation canals in the area. The company, like several others created about the same time, tried to channel the waters of the Payette River to the various farms of its members. However, the firm suffered through the typical shortage of funds, questionable engineering, and quick construction. Many of these canals had to be rebuilt over the years, and their conditions led many to be called ditches instead of canals.

Just east of this canal, the railroad, which is running east-west, turns to the northeast to enter the Black Canyon of the Payette River.

**31.8** **PLAZA** – This was a 1980-foot siding in 1976; it was 2749 feet long in 1932. Nothing besides the mainline seems to be here today. In 1948, Plaza was a flag stop for the passenger trains, with #385 at 10:40am and #386 at 2:35pm. The railroad is climbing as it heads north at a grade of 0.8%.

Just uphill to the east is the Black Canyon Canal that the railroad crossed while coming down Freezeout Hill. In this area, the railroad leaves Emmett Valley, a wide and fertile valley used for farming and ranching. Heading north, the country becomes more mountainous and the timber industry became the dominant employer and rail shipper until the railroad reaches Smiths Ferry, where the Long Valley introduced livestock to the shipment mix.

**Picket's Corral**

To the east of Plaza and in the low hills is the famous Picket's Corral, at one time an infamous roadhouse. Picket's Corral started as a simple cabin made from driftwood, whose owners provided meals and lodging. For protection, the cabin was built with a series of tunnels that led to the livestock corrals. These tunnels reportedly could be used to hold animals to protect them from the Indians.

Soon after Emmett Valley was settled during the 1860s, a gang of outlaws began robbing settlers and stealing horses and livestock. One of the leaders of the gang was David C. Updyke, sheriff of Ada County, which Emmett was in at the time. With no law enforcement willing to help, a number of ranchers, farmers and local businessmen organized to protect their property.

At one of the meetings, efforts were organized as the Vigilance Committee of Payette Valley and William "Poker Bill" McConnell, of Horseshoe Bend, was selected as captain. It should be noted that McConnell was later a U.S. Marshall, an Idaho Constitution Convention delegate, governor of Idaho, U.S. Senator, U.S. Immigration commissioner and inspection officer for Indian Affairs, and he held a number of other jobs of importance in the region.

At the meeting, it was announced that a legal process was created for handling the criminals. Reportedly, any criminal caught would have a fair trial by a jury of seven members, with the majority vote to determine the verdict. Three forms of punishment were authorized: (1) 24 hours to leave the country; (2) whipping in public; or (3) death.

With several direct confrontations taking place, some from the Picket Corral gang left the region. However, Sheriff Updyk attempted to break the Vigilance Committee by issuing warrants against them. However, hearings in Boise found that no charges could be found and the vigilantes were released. After several shootings, Updyke and at least one of his men were caught and hanged. It is interesting that several of the outlaws who fled the area were later hanged for offenses in other parts of the West.

**33.0 BLACK CANYON** – As the railroad curves into Black Canyon, note the small dam in the Payette River that moves water into the Last Chance Canal. The railroad then passes Cobblestone Park, managed by the U.S. Department of Interior's Bureau of Reclamation. The park marks where the Black Canyon spur track once was located. The 5-car spur was located here for loads destined to area shippers and for construction of the dam. Look for the dirt road that crosses the tracks at the location of the spur track.

Black Canyon Reservoir is to the west, created from the Payette River. The designed water level is at an elevation of 2497 feet above sea level. The dam was built between 1922 and 1924 at a cost of $1,500,000, then re-constructed between 1951 and 1955 by the United States Bureau of Reclamation. The dam is 183 feet high and provides water for the Black Canyon Canal, which currently waters approximately 58,250 acres of Boise and Payette valley farms. There is also a power plant at Black Canyon Dam which generates electricity for commercial use as well as for irrigation pumping. However, the dam ended salmon fishing on the Payette River as it blocked the spawning route up the Payette River.

Although the railroad was built through the area first, it was not moved for the lake. Instead, the property had already been acquired and marked out for the reservoir and the Idaho Northern had to avoid it. The line enters the Payette River canyon and the track starts an almost continuous curve from here to Cascade.

**33.2 BLACK CANYON CANAL BRIDGE** – The irrigation canal starts at the Black Canyon Diversion Dam, and the railroad crosses it using a 50-foot deck plate girder span. Many Union Pacific documents show this to be the Gay Canal.

If you look to the northwest, the visible peak is Little Butte at 3494 feet high. The railroad will soon be at an elevation higher than this peak.

**33.3 TUNNEL NO. 2** – This is a 486-foot tunnel, with 254 feet lined with timber. Did you find Tunnel Number 1? It doesn't even show on old track charts. However, there were once plans for a Tunnel No. 1, but a change in the plans for the route eliminated the need for the tunnel. North of Tunnel No. 2, the railroad runs right on the bank of Black Canyon Reservoir, using curve after curve to do the job.

Tunnel No. 2 effectively divides the farmlands to the west, and the mountains to the east. It is also a scenic location with the Black Canyon Reservoir immediately next to the tracks. Photo by Barton Jennings.

**36.6 ANDERSON CREEK BRIDGE** – This stream is crossed on a curving 180-foot (six 30-foot spans) steel pile trestle bridge, located in the middle of a horseshoe curve. Anderson Creek forms on the west side of Crown Point at an elevation of about 4600 feet. It flows to the west and then north to here, picking up several smaller streams along the way. During the 1870s, there was some successful placer mining of gold along the creek.

Across the lake is Triangle Park, one of several parks that are part of the Bureau of Reclamation's public outreach. It is located on Idaho Highway 52, which runs on the other shore of Black Canyon Reservoir. The elevation here is 2516 feet.

**38.5 TUNNEL NO. 3** – This short tunnel is 129 feet long, and has traditionally been lined with timber. The soils above the tunnel are not solid, and the tunnel has historically been a challenge to maintain. The tunnel is used to cut a corner on the Payette River as the railroad turns sharply to the south.

The Payette River is forced to make several tight turns in this area to get around Regan Butte, clearly visible to the east as a train exits Tunnel No. 3 when heading toward Cascade. Regan Butte has an elevation of 3310 feet.

Tunnel No. 3 is used as a shortcut around a bend of the Payette River. As can be seen, the hills are still dry and treeless in this area. Photo by Barton Jennings.

Tunnel No. 3 is short and passes through a sandy ridge, requiring a timber lining. This northbound train demonstrates how high the ridge is and why a tunnel was used instead of a cut. Photo by Barton Jennings.

TunnelNo. 3. Photo by Barton Jennings.

**39.4 JOHNSON CREEK BRIDGE** – Look for the six-span timber pile trestle bridge. Johnson Creek starts in the mountains to the south, just over a ridge to the east of Anderson Creek. Union Pacific documents show that this is Cherry Creek, named for the many choke cherries in the area.

To the south and up Johnson Creek is the Johnson Creek Mine. The mine has never produced enough product to be worked, but it has been evaluated several times. The mine is considered to be mainly a rare-earth element (REE) deposit. A rare-earth element is one of a set of seventeen chemical elements in the periodic table, often needed for modern batteries, computers, and other electrical devices. These include cerium (Ce), dysprosium (Dy), erbium (Er), europium (Eu), gadolinium (Gd), holmium (Ho), lanthanum (La), lutetium (Lu), neodymium (Nd), praseodymium (Pr), promethium (Pm), samarium (Sm), scandium (Sc), terbium (Tb), thulium (Tm), ytterbium (Yb), and yttrium (Y). The reason that the deposits were examined is that the area was prospected for gold with some minor success.

Not far to the east, the railroad cuts away from the Payette River to pass through the former town of Montour, located in Montour Valley. This also allowed the railroad to avoid a large loop of the river.

**41.1 MONTOUR (MR)** – Montour is the location of a siding that is 2035 feet long. There was also at one time a nice two-story depot, located where Montour Road crosses the tracks. During 1948, Montour was a scheduled passenger train stop, with #385 at 11:20am and #386 at 1:55pm. Montour was also once the location of one of ten railroad stockyards on the line; this location featured four pens. Finally, there were section houses here for the track gang that worked the track north to the Hell Roaring Gulch Bridge at Milepost 52.3.

This area has long been a popular location for fishing and hunting, with archaeological evidence of a buried pit house and other artifacts, indicating use as long ago as 5000 years. The first major white occupation occurred in the early 1860s when gold was discovered in the area. The land went through a number of owners, but eventually William Mitchell homesteaded 196 acres, and his brother-in-law Edson Marsh homesteaded 404 acres nearby. Combined, the two properties became known as the Mitchell-Marsh Ranch.

The location of Montour became important when a mail and stage route was established through the area, and the ranch became a way station known as Marsh. The area began to grow, and in 1871, Mitchell established a post office with the name Squaw Creek. In 1882, Mitchell and Marsh opened a ferry on the Payette River at Squaw Creek, meeting the demand of fortune hunters heading to and from the Squaw Creek diggings. On June 14, 1889, Edson Marsh became the new postmaster, and the post office and community were renamed Marsh. However, the early boom of the community didn't last long and the post office closed in November 1906.

The area became ranch land, part of the Edson Marsh-John Ireton Ranch. As the Idaho Northern Railway was being built north from Emmett, the railroad passed through the former townsite. E. H. Dewey, president and general manager of the railroad, decided that the location could be a good station location. A townsite was platted, using the name Montour. There is a great deal of confusion about the source of the name. One source says that the name Montour was chosen by Dewey's secretary, who said that the word was French and expressed the magnificent view from this point. However, another version states that the word was chosen because it means "a frame" or "a setting," describing the location's pleasant environment or setting. A third version states that a Mr. Montour was an investor in the various businesses run by the Dewey family.

Montour never became the city that Dewey projected, and it remained a small town. The Montour Precinct had a population of 219 in 1930, 172 in 1940, and 157 in 1950. The construction of the Black Canyon Diversion Dam changed the water flow in the nearby Payette River, leading to a series of floods around the town. To reduce the damage, the Bureau of Reclamation bought out the property owners in the 1970s. Much of the area is now the Montour Wildlife Management Area, maintained by the Idaho Department of Fish and Game. Heading north up the Payette River, pretty much all of the land around the railroad from here on is either state, Bureau of Land Management (BLM), or National Forest federal land. In Idaho, 62% of the land is owned by the federal government.

## Idaho Northern Branch – Emmett to Cascade

Northbound IN&P #4506 passes the siding and station sign at Montour, Idaho. This locomotive, like all of those used by the railroad, was acquired secondhand. This GP40 locomotive was built in September 1967 as Louisville & Nashville #3012. It later became Seaboard System #6808, and then CSX #6808. It has since been sold and now operates as Copper Basin #302, based at Hayden, Arizona. Photos by Barton Jennings.

This photo was made as part of the Historic American Buildings Survey and shows a typical tool house used by section forces on the Idaho Northern Branch. Historic American Buildings Survey, Creator. *Idaho Northern Railroad, Tool Shed, North Broadway Street, West side, Montour, Gem County Idaho.* Montour, Gem County, Idaho. 1933. Documentation Compiled After. Library of Congress, https://www.loc.gov/item/id0057/.

**42.3 LARKIN** – This is a retired side track, once a 300-foot spur track. Union Pacific records also show that in 1930, there was a freight platform on the east side of the tracks. The name Larkin was common in the area. Look for the private ranch road grade crossing.

**44.9 ROCK CREEK BRIDGE** – It takes several small bridges in about 300 feet to cross the creek. Most of the time the stream is dry, but it can be wet during the spring snow melt or after a heavy rain. The creek closely follows the county line until it turns west to its source on the east side of Crown Point.

**45.0 COUNTY LINE** – To the west, the railroad has been in **Gem County**. To the east is **Boise County**, one of the most rural counties in the state. The county, named for the Boise River (named by French-Canadian explorers for the various types of trees along the river), was created by the Washington Territory on February 4, 1864, making it one of the oldest counties in the Territory, and one of the original Idaho counties. However, today it is much smaller than its original size. The county seat is Idaho City, but Horseshoe Bend is its largest city. The total population of the almost 2000-square mile county was 7028 in the 2010 census.

As the railroad enters Boise County, it passes the lowest spot in the county at 2572 feet. Heading up the Payette River, the railroad will often be squeezed between the river and the surrounding slopes of the river gorge.

**49.2 PAYETTE RIVER BRIDGE** – The railroad crosses the Payette River using a 90-foot through plate girder span, and a 125-foot Pratt through truss span. The bridge was shown in company timetables as being an obstruction to train crewmen riding the top or sides of trains. This bridge was also a cited reason why the maximum class of steam locomotive on the Idaho Northern Branch was a Class 560 Consolidation (2-8-0). As many as four of these locomotives would be used on a single train, spaced throughout the train to reduce the weight loading as they crossed the bridge.

In the 85 miles of the Payette River, it varies from being a mountain stream with Class IV rafting runs, to a flat irrigation river providing water to the adjacent farmland just before it flows into the Snake River. Near Banks, Idaho, the river splits into the North Fork and the South Fork. The North Fork starts more than 100 miles to the north in the Salmon Mountains. It is dammed several times en route, creating several large lakes. This is the branch that the Idaho Northern Railway followed. Heading to the east at Banks is the South Fork Payette River, which forms in the Sawtooth Wilderness of the Sawtooth National Recreation Area. The South Fork is about 80 miles long and splits with the Middle Fork in Garden Valley.

Historically, the river was used by roaming bands of Native American tribes, including the Shoshone, Nez Perce, and Paiute. The tribes hunted, fished, and collected plants along the route. The tribes routinely burned the area to encourage the growth of the plants they wanted and to keep their campsites clear. Many of these clearings became trading posts, created by the French-Canadian employees of the North West Company. The name of the Payette River comes from one of these employees, Francois Payette. Payette later headed the Hudson Bay Company's Fort Boise trading post on the Snake River.

Logging along the upper length of the river boomed in the early 1900s with the arrival of the railroad. However, changing policies in the National Forests, the lack of private land, and the availability of lower cost timber elsewhere led to a decline in the industry. Today, ranching and recreation lead the activity lists on the upper reaches, while farming and ranching still lead on the lower part of the river.

**49.4 POWER CANAL BRIDGE** – The railroad uses an 80-foot three-span deck plate girder bridge to cross this canal. In 1932, this bridge was listed as an obstruction to train crewmen riding the top or sides of trains. At the time it was a 65-foot through plate girder span. However, the bridge was replaced when the canal was upgraded. Unlike most of the canals, this one is not used for irrigation, but instead for electrical power production. This is a run-of-river hydroelectric facility, where water is channeled down a canal, through a powerhouse, and back into the river without the need of creating a dam and lake.

A low diversion dam sends part of the Payette River down this canal, which ends more than four miles downstream at a powerhouse. The first hydroelectric project was built here by 1902 and operated until 1954. After that, the powerhouse and canal sat unused, with the canal filling with sediment and vegetation. The powerhouse and canal were reactivated during the 1990s by the Horseshoe Bend Hydroelectric Company. Work was done to enlarge and increase the depth of the intake canal so a larger generating system could be used at the powerhouse.

Power was again produced starting in 1995, using two Kaplan turbines producing 9.5 megawatts of electricity, enough "to fill the needs in electricity of more than 2,850 households in Idaho." Innergex, a global company involved in the renewable energy sector, acquired the facility in 2004. They own run-of-river hydroelectric facilities, wind farms, solar photovoltaic farms and geothermal power generation plants around the world.

**49.7 HORSESHOE BEND (HB)** – This is a 1485-foot long siding at 2614 feet above sea level. There is also a short siding to the north (railroad-west) and a spur to the south. There is also a small station and museum complex from when Horseshoe Bend was the base of operations for excursion train operations over the Idaho Northern & Pacific; the Thunder Mountain Railroad.

The railroad reached the north bank here in 1912 and built a two-story depot and called it Horseshoe Bend. The station is now located on the north bank of the Payette River and serves as a bed and breakfast, the Riverside Restaurant & Depot Inn along Highway 55. The depot has been described as a frame structure with the center, two-story section measuring 24 feet by 21 feet. Each one-story wing measured 24 feet by 12 feet. This seems to be a common design used at many locations along the line.

With the railroad's arrival, the town crossed the river and became a center for the livestock business including horses, cattle and sheep. In 1948, train #385 departed Horseshoe Bend at 11:55am on its trip northward, while train #386 was scheduled to depart at 1:30pm. There used to be a 50,000-gallon water tank for steam locomotives at Horseshoe Bend. It used the Payette River as a water source.

Reportedly, the first settler in the Horseshoe Bend area was Mahlon B. Moore who arrived in 1862-1863 as part of a regional gold prospecting boom. Gold was discovered in 1862 in the Boise Basin mountains to the east, near Idaho City. By the time prospectors arrived, winter was closing in, so many miners temporarily settled here, waiting for snows to thaw at the higher elevations. Several names were initially used for the area including The Big Bend and The Bend. Later a town on the south bank took the name Warrinersville after Benjamin Warriner, who became the first postmaster there in October 1865 (he may have gotten the job because records indicate that he also built the post office). Warriner also operated a local sawmill, one of the first in the area.

The post office was renamed Horseshoe Bend (or Horse Shoe Bend on some documents) on September 11, 1867. The name came from the huge bend in the Payette River, and the railroad also makes a big curve here. For the river, it basically makes a turn of more than 90 degrees from flowing south to flowing west. The bend provided a small but flat area perfect for settlement.

A number of roads were built from Horseshoe Bend to reach the surrounding gold fields, communities, and timber. Felix Harris built a toll road between Horseshoe Bend and the Boise Basin that avoided the steep climb over Porter Creek. This toll road was still in operation as late as 1906. As part of an agreement to cut National Forest timber, the Payette Lumber Company built a wagon road in 1908 from Horseshoe Bend to Smiths Ferry through the canyon of the Payette River. At the time, most logging still used ox teams and rivers, and logs were often moved on the river during high water levels to the Horseshoe Bend sawmill.

As the community grew, the area was heavily used to winter livestock for the wagon and mule trains serving the nearby mines. This activity later turned into a great stock business for the new railroad. Another gold rush happened when gold was found in the area in 1890. Railroad surveyors arrived about 1910. The railroad arrived by 1913, creating another economic boom in the community. Several sawmills were built in the area to take advantage of the transportation. There was also a single-pen railroad stockyard here.

On April 14, 1947, Horseshoe Bend became an incorporated village. On May 9, 1967, the village reorganized to become a city. For years, Horseshoe Bend supported local ranchers, loggers and miners. However, on September 30, 1998, the city's primary employer, Boise Cascade, closed its sawmill. Even with that bad economic news, Horseshoe Bend is still the largest city in Boise County, with a population of 707 during the 2010 census.

Today, Horseshoe Bend is a center of the Payette River rafting industry, with cafes, rafting companies, and just about any service the outdoor enthusiast could desire. The whitewater business is a big part of Idaho's economy. Idaho has almost 3500 miles of whitewater rivers, more than any other state (California and Maine are the only two other states that even approach 3000 miles). The Payette River provides everything from easy, family-oriented floats (main channel of the Payette), to a good mix of whitewater (South Fork), to world-class advanced

## Idaho Northern Branch – Emmett to Cascade

whitewater on the North Fork (more than 20 class IV and V rapids in 16 miles).

Highway 52 (which has been following the railroad since Payette and on the north bank of the Payette River for the last few miles) and Highway 55 (which runs from Nampa, around the west side of Boise, and then follows the railroad on to Cascade and then McCall) meet here. Highway 55 between Boise and McCall (and on to New Meadows) is designated as the Payette River Scenic Byway. This junction of roads provides the closest good access to the Payette River from Boise and Interstate 84.

For a number of years, the railroad operated the Thunder Mountain Line, an excursion train, out of Horseshoe Bend. Because of this, and past industries, there were a number of tracks and passenger facilities here. Photo by Barton Jennings.

The Thunder Mountain Line had their own power, including former Gulf, Mobile & Ohio F3, which had been rebuilt into what was called an F10. This became Idaho Northern & Pacific #1112. Photo by Barton Jennings.

**The Lumber Business**

Lumber has been a big business at Horseshoe Bend almost since its founding. The community's first name, Warrinersville, came from the operator, Benjamin Warriner, of one of the first sawmills in the area. The lumber business was local until the railroad arrived, and soon a larger mill was built here.

During the early 1900s, the Payette Lumber Company was cutting some timber in the area. The Harris Lumber Company had a sawmill, but according to the *American Machinist*, it burned at a total loss late in 1918. In 1938, the Hoff Company became a partner in a Horseshoe Bend sawmill. It bought the mill in 1940, creating the Hoff Lumber Company. The firm then opened a molding plant built next to the Horseshoe Bend sawmill as Hoff Forest Products in 1956. In 1975, the sawmill and molding plant were sold to Boise Cascade. The sawmill became the largest mill along this part of the Payette River. With the move to cutting regrowth timber, Boise Cascade spent $5 million to upgrade the Horseshoe Bend mill in 1989 so it could handle small-diameter logs. However, the national economy and changes in timber demand and sources led Boise Cascade to close the mill on September 30, 1998. The mill has been removed, and the lumber mill land to the south of the railroad has been prepared for redevelopment.

**51.7 IDAHO HIGHWAY 55** – The railroad passes under Idaho Highway 55. This road extends from a junction with U.S. Highway 95 at Marsing, to another junction with U.S. Highway 95 at New Meadows, 150 miles apart. A major feature of the highway is the trip up the Payette River and its North Fork.

Just south of the overpass is the former location of the Caldwell Lumber Company sawmill, marked by the large millpond between the tracks and the Payette River. In 1944, J. R. Simplot organized the Caldwell Lumber Company and bought this sawmill. The firm added a planing mill and a presto log shaping facility to use waste from the mill. The company held a number of timber contracts in the area, but let them lapse after some logging in 1957. A report from the National Forest Service stated that the "Petitioner began cutting operations pursuant to the contracts, but in 1957, due to a lack of timber in the vicinity of the Horseshoe Bend sawmill and because of the adverse conditions of the lumber market, it commenced the liquidation of its logging equipment and cut down its production at the sawmill.... In the fiscal year ended February 28, 1958, petitioner's Horseshoe Bend sawmill was sold and no further lumber manufacturing was done by petitioner in Idaho."

Just north of the highway overpass, a low water dam can be seen in the river, made of native stone. The dam once forced water into a canal to power the sawmill.

**52.4 HELL ROARING GULCH BRIDGE** – This looks to be a small, insignificant 20-foot beam open deck bridge, but what a name for a western location. The snow melt each spring explains the name. It is easy to tell that at times the stream moves a great deal of water, rock and soil by looking at the large alluvial fan in the Payette River. An alluvial fan is debris that has been deposited where a stream flows into a larger body of water.

**53.7 CALAMITY GULCH BRIDGE** – This is another small bridge, a 20-foot steel pile trestle, across a creek with an interesting name.

Across the Payette River is Mount Maria, peaking at 3472 feet. To its north is Jerusalem Valley, reportedly named by Reverend Fred Faull in 1864. There were some minor coal mines in the area, a part of the Horseshoe Bend Coal District. A post office with the name Jerusalem was here 1885-1888.

In this area, the railroad operates on a narrow shelf alongside the river, with tall hillsides above. Along the river grow trees and other vegetation, while the hillsides are still dry. Photo by Barton Jennings.

Photos by Barton Jennings.

**55.1 GARDENA** – Look for the 1485-foot siding to the east. This is Gardena, an unincorporated community in Boise County. Officials of the Oregon Short Line Railroad named this site in 1914 in an effort to make it sound attractive to potential settlers. This is another former livestock location as well as a small community which provided supplies for area ranches. The elevation is 2684 feet above sea level.

Gardena has seen some recent growth as the Payette River has become a tourist destination. There are a number of houses here, built alongside the west side of the river. Gardena has the advantage of having a bridge across the river – Brownlee Road. The community of Brownlee is located in the mountains to the west. It has been described as a small mining community created in the late 19th century.

Although Gardena was a planned community created by the railroad, it was only a flag stop in 1948. However, at least one of the passenger trains stopped each day as the two passenger trains were scheduled to meet here at 12:40pm.

55.2 **BROWNLEE CREEK BRIDGE** – This stream starts on the north side of the mining community of Brownlee. Some sources state that the creek and town was named for J. Brownlee, an Idaho City miner. The railroad crosses the stream on a five-span timber pile trestle.

57.1 **BOULDER CREEK BRIDGE** – This is another three-span timber pile trestle that carries snow melt and rainwater off the generally dry hillsides to the west. Across the river are several rafting centers which provide raft and kayak trips down parts of the Payette River.

62.5 **DRY BUCK CREEK BRIDGE** – A 3-span, 90-foot steel pile trestle crosses this eight-mile long creek which starts on Dry Buck Mountain. The name originates from the Dry Buck band of the Shoshoni who inhabited the Horseshoe Bend area. They were gone by 1880. Heading north, the Payette River Valley becomes more vegetated as it climbs in altitude.

**64.1 BANKS (AB)** – Because steep grades start north of here, Banks was at one time an important, yet isolated railroad town. A two-story depot, a stockyard pen, a section house, crew quarters, locomotive facilities, and all of the necessary related structures were built here to handle the crews and pusher engines for the steep grades north of here. There was also a restaurant here at the Canyon Hotel to serve passengers off of the daily trains. The northbound #385 mixed train was scheduled to leave here in 1948 at 1:30pm, meaning that it had 95 minutes to travel the 14 miles between Horseshoe Bend and Banks, to switch local customers, and to grab a bite to eat. Southbound (eastbound in the timetables of the time) #386 departed at 12:05pm after its passengers and crew also had a chance for a quick meal. This train had 70 minutes to travel from Big Eddy, just 11 miles away, plus switch at Banks.

During steam days, Banks was generally assigned several helper locomotives to assist with the movement of trains from here to Cascade. A 65-foot hand-operated turntable, and fuel and water facilities were maintained at Banks for these helpers. Banks was clearly noted in employee timetables as having clearance issues due to a water tank spout and a coal platform. The 50,000-gallon water tower used the river as its water source. There was also a 40-ton platform with an air hoist that served as a coal dock. For a number of years, there was also a two-stall engine house, each stall being 79 feet long. These facilities were removed during the early 1950s when diesel locomotives began to be used on the branch.

Union Pacific Idaho Division timetables such as #126 of September 18, 1932, indicated other uses for Banks. One of the operating instructions stated that all eastbound (southbound) "freight and mixed trains will stop at Big Eddy, Mains and Banks for inspection of train and to permit wheels to cool." This inspection was needed because the same timetable stated "All retainers must be used at MP 80 to MP 64, Idaho Northern Branch." A retainer is a part of the brake system that can be set by hand. When on, it prevents the brakes from coming completely off, meaning that the brakes are at least slowing the train, even when going downhill.

Unfortunately, with the coming of the diesel locomotive, the structures were removed and Banks no longer has the feel of a railroad town, although it has been heavily used by the Idaho Northern & Pacific to meet and split trains. Today, Banks marks the dividing line between the Idaho and Cascade Subdivisions of the Idaho Northern & Pacific. Located at an elevation of 2809 feet above sea level, the railroad built a pavilion shelter here for the operation of the *Thunder Mountain Line* passenger trains. There is also still a 1650-foot siding at Banks.

While little remains of the railroad town, Banks has seen some recent growth due to tourism and the construction of vacation, retirement, and other homes. Banks has become a rafting community with a number of businesses dependent upon the rafting industry. The Idaho Transportation Department has a Division of Highway Maintenance Station just north of Banks where Banks Grade Road bridges the

Payette River. In the same area is the Banks River Access, used by rafters and kayakers.

The Payette River splits here, with the tracks now following the North Fork Payette River heading north. Some sources show that the Payette River begins here, while others show that the Payette River begins to the east where the South Fork and Middle Fork come together. No matter the definition, the river becomes more narrow and wilder as the railroad heads north.

Merle Banks obtained 160 acres here in 1908 using the Forest Homestead Act of 1906, which opened agricultural lands in national forests for settlement. It took several years for Banks to comply with the law as he had to actually grow crops. Merle Banks was a rancher who provided a right-of-way for the railroad as part of a plan to create facilities for area livestock.

Today, Banks is an unincorporated community with a population of 17 during the 2010 census. Even with the small population, there is a post office. The post office was the source of the town's name, as it was named for the Banks family. Besides Merle Banks, W. B. Banks was another local rancher and Emma Banks was the first postmaster when the post office opened on June 5, 1914.

IN&P #4506 is heading north as it passes a former section house at Banks. Photo by Barton Jennings.

Because Banks was the last wide spot on the railroad for a quite a few miles, there were a number of railroad facilities here. In 2003, there were several small buildings that had been used by the track forces. Photo by Barton Jennings.

**65.1 PHILLIPS CREEK BRIDGE** – Northbound grades of 2.26% up to 2.50% start here as the railroad crosses a 30-foot steel pile trestle. Phillips Creek forms on the southeast side of Dry Buck Mountain, and flows to the southeast. In 1939, a 1200-acre fire along Phillips Creek was the largest fire in the Boise National Forest that year.

**66.8 NORTH FORK PAYETTE RIVER BRIDGE** – This bridge provides some great views of the North Fork Payette River as the railroad crosses over from the west bank to the east bank of the river. The bridge was built in 1912 by the American Bridge Company of New York. From south to north, there are two 50-foot deck plate girder spans, two 138-foot Warren deck truss spans, and then two more 50-foot deck plate girder spans. Many sources state that these are the only Warren deck truss spans in Idaho. The total length of the bridge is 484 feet.

The North Fork Payette River bridge is unique in Idaho, featuring several Warren deck truss spans. With a road under the north end of the bridge, photos are possible from both sides of the structure. Photos by Barton Jennings.

Photo by Barton Jennings.

## Idaho Northern Branch – Emmett to Cascade

Photo by Barton Jennings.

**67.5 IDAHO HIGHWAY 55 BRIDGE** – The railroad uses a curved through plate girder bridge to cross Highway 55 as the road crosses the North Fork Payette River.

**69.3 MAINS** – Mains was another location designated in the Union Pacific *Idaho Division Time-Table 126* (September 18, 1932), where all eastbound (southbound) freight and mixed trains were to stop "for inspection of train and to permit wheels to cool." At the time, there was a 587-foot siding here. Mains was not listed as a station by 1948.

Mains was the limit between the track section gang based at Banks and the gang based at Smiths Ferry. The North Fork Range is to the east and Dry Buck Mountain is to the west.

As the Idaho Northern Branch was being built, Guy B. Mains was a forest supervisor for much of the national forest land that the railroad passed through. Guy B. Mains was born into a logging family in Wisconsin and he moved west when the timber was used up. He worked for the Barber Lumber Company in Idaho, and then became a forest supervisor for the U.S. Forest Service. He was the supervisor of the Boise National Forest from 1925 until 1940. The Payette National Forest was officially created on April 1, 1944, with Mains as the first supervisor. Despite the titles he held, Guy B. Mains may be best known for helping to create a unified fire-fighting program between various timber companies, and state and federal land owners, known as the Southern Idaho Timber Protective Association.

**70.7 HOWELL CREEK BRIDGE** – This is a 30-foot-long, three span, steel pile open deck trestle. Howell Creek forms to the northeast in the North Fork Range, at an elevation of more than 6000 feet.

Just south of here, Valley County comes in from the west, and the Payette River is the county line. With the railroad along the east shore, it stays in Boise County.

**72.8 FARRELL** – This area is basically one of the roughest whitewater stretches around, with a long series of Class V rapids on the adjacent North Fork Payette River.

Farrell was not a common name in the area, although John O'Farrell is considered the founder of Boise, having built the first home in the area in 1863. A map from 1940 does not show a community in the area with the name Farrell, but it does show a large amount of the land to the east of the river belonging to Andrew Little. As the story goes, Scottish-born Andrew Little came to Idaho in 1884 with two dogs and $25. He quickly invested in land and sheep, becoming the largest sheep operator in Idaho and one of the largest in the nation. Known as "The Idaho Sheep King," Andrew is credited with owning 100,000 head of sheep and marketing a million pounds of wool a year by 1929. He owned pieces of land all along the railroad from Payette to McCall and employed as many as 400 men.

In 1932, there was a 517-foot spur track here. There was also a freight platform at the time. The February 29, 1948, Union Pacific Idaho Division employee timetable did not list Farrell as a station.

**75.2 BIG EDDY** – Big Eddy is another small station that once played a major role on the railroad, and there is still a siding to the east that is 1155 feet long. According to the September 18, 1932, Union Pacific Idaho Division timetable, all eastbound (southbound) freight and mixed trains were to stop at Big Eddy for inspection of the train and to permit the wheels to cool. There was a 50,000-gallon water tank here that the locomotives could use during the stop. The railroad used the Payette River to supply the water tank. While the tank is gone, the footings of the tower can still be found.

The name Big Eddy came about because loggers built a splash dam across the river, creating some slack water where they could collect logs being floated down the river. The station was at an elevation of 4089 feet above sea level. Across the river is the Big Eddy Campground, operated by the Boise National Forest. Located between the Payette River and Idaho Highway 55, it is one of four along the North Fork of the Payette River between Banks and Smiths Ferry. Whitewater rafting and kayaking are popular activities here, and anglers enjoy excellent fishing for whitefish and rainbow trout.

To the east is Packer John Mountain (elevation 7056 feet), which has a peak summit that runs north-south, and was once the home of a fire lookout. Just some foundations remain today of the fire tower that was built in 1914. The mountain was named for "Packer John" Welch, who hauled supplies between Lewiston and Idaho City during the Boise Basin Gold Rush of 1863-1864. Just south of the south switch at Big Eddy is a suspension footbridge that crosses the river.

In 1948, train #385 was available to be flagged at 2:20pm on its trip northward, while train #386 was scheduled to pass the station at 10:55am. Big Eddy is a short relatively flat location, with a grade of only 0.37%, with grades of 2.5% to both the north and the south.

The suspension footbridge south of the Big Eddy Campground allows access to both sides of the river for fishing and photography. Photo by Barton Jennings.

With Idaho Highway 55 on the west side of the Payette River, and the railroad to the east, a number of good photos are possible in this area. Photo by Barton Jennings.

**76.9 COUNTY LINE** – To the south is **Boise County**, while to the north is **Valley County**, the fifth largest county in Idaho at 3665 square miles of territory. **Valley County** is named for Long Valley, a rich wide valley that follows the North Fork Payette River from Cascade to McCall. When white prospectors and settlers entered the area during the early 1800s, the valley was a home of the Tukudeka, or Sheep Eaters, a branch of the Shoshone. This tribe was known for living in the high mountains of the region, including the Yellowstone area. Their name came from them sharing the pastures of the bighorn sheep, and their use of the sheep for food.

Gold was found in the area during the early 1860s, and the tribe was soon gone. Several small communities were formed as relay stations for the freight wagons, and as mines played out and miners became farmers. The first post office in the county opened at VanWyck in 1888, and the next year, Tom McCall took squatter's rights on Payette Lake, leading to the city of McCall. A conflict started when the area began to be used as summer pasture for livestock from the Boise Valley. Local residents several times slaughtered herds to push the ranchers out of the valley, but it was another gold strike and the arrival of the railroad that really changed the area.

William H. Dewey arrived in the area after an 1893 gold strike in the Thunder Mountain area. By 1902, Dewey was operating a major gold mining operation. Warren Dredge Company opened a sawmill on Payette Lake in 1896 to meet the need for mining timbers and lumber for housing. With Dewey's interest in the area, he soon funded the construction of a railroad up the Payette River. The Oregon Short Line built into McCall in 1914, and it had an immediate impact as some towns off the railroad, like Alpha, Crawford and Roseberry, soon died, while others on the railroad, like Cascade, Donnelly and McCall, grew.

Logging quickly grew with the railroad, and sawmills opened throughout the area. The railroad also allowed ranching and farming to become more profitable. This growth led to the creation of Valley County on February 26, 1917, from parts of Boise and Idaho counties. In 1948, much of Long Valley was flooded with the completion of the Cascade Dam, designed to provide irrigation water and for flood control. The main highway and railroad had to be moved. Additionally, much of the best farm and ranch land was lost. However, the area gained Lake Cascade and all of its related fishing and water recreation activities. The last two major sawmills also closed toward the end of the 20th Century – Boise Cascade's McCall mill in October 1977, and their Cascade mill in May 2001.

Today, Cascade is the county seat of Valley County, but McCall is the largest city. The population in 2010 was 9862 people. It is also the home of the endangered Idaho ground squirrel.

77.3 **TUNNEL NO. 4** – This is a 221-foot tunnel, lined with timber, that allows the railroad to avoid a sharp turn of the river.

Tunnel No. 4 is another short timber-lined tunnel, built through a soft and sandy ridge at a bend in the river. Photo by Barton Jennings.

**80.3 BEAVER CREEK BRIDGE** – The name Beaver is used throughout Idaho since it was fur-trapping country in the early 1800s. Someone evidently found a few up this creek, crossed by the railroad using a 20-foot beam open deck span.

This was another location that was commonly referenced in Union Pacific timetables. One instruction was that "All retainers must be used at MP 80 to MP 64, Idaho Northern Branch." Additionally, southbound passenger trains were required to conduct an air brake test here. Trains that stopped could take advantage of a small 6000-gallon water tank, whose spout was cited as an obstruction to crewmen riding the top and sides of trains.

The Beaver Creek area was another wide spot in the river that provided a rare flat area on the railroad. This view shows how different it is from the areas just to the south. Photo by Barton Jennings.

**82.7 SMITHS FERRY (SF)** – Smiths Ferry began about 1887 when a ferry was built across the river by Clinton Meyers. The purpose of the ferry was to move livestock to and from their summer pasture, but freighters, miners, and others also used the ferry. In 1891, the ferry was sold to Jim (James) Smith, and as the community grew, the location became known as Smith's Ferry, simplified to Smiths Ferry.

The area also grew thanks to the construction of the Oregon Short Line. The company Coe & Carter had been running tie yards for Union Pacific in Wyoming, and was involved in supplying ties to the new railroad. The company set up logging camps along the North Fork of the Payette River, including at Smiths Ferry. There, they hired hundreds of men to cut ties and then to float them down the river. In 1902, the Payette Lumber & Manufacturing Company acquired more than 30,000 acres of state timber in Long Valley. The company chose Smiths Ferry for the location of a splash dam as a control point along the river. The logs were moved from dam to dam down the Payette River to several mills. Even after the timber was cut, most of the land in the area in 1940 was shown to belong to the Boise Payette Lumber Company, and was identified as "reforestation land." Across the river to the west, the distinctive landmark is Cougar Mountain (5361 feet of elevation).

With all of the activity in the area, a post office using the name Fern was located about two miles upstream beginning on May 23, 1902. The post office was renamed Smiths Ferry on February 17, 1913. The post office closed on May 22, 1964. Today, Smiths Ferry has a population of approximately

100, and is another area community experiencing growth due to tourism in the region.

**The Railroad at Smiths Ferry**

Smiths Ferry was a busy location for the railroad, and was located at an elevation of 4538 feet. It is situated in a relatively flat spot after miles of hard climbing – the steepest grades end about two miles south of here. Because of these grades, passenger trains, freight trains, and mixed trains all were required to conduct an air brake test at Smiths Ferry.

Grading on the railroad reached here in 1912 and trains were running in 1913. The railroad built a two-story, wood frame depot, with housing for the agent on the second floor (a common design on the line). There is a 1430-foot siding to the west, and there were once a number of other tracks measuring more than 1200 feet long. There is also a wye once used for helper engines, located to the north of the siding. During the 1930s, there was a four-pen stockyard here to handle the livestock business. There were also section houses here for the track gang which maintained the line between mileposts 69.3 and 84.3. Several boxcars were used for maintenance buildings.

In 1948, Train #385 departed Smiths Ferry at 3:00pm, while train #386 was scheduled to depart at 10:25am.

Smiths Ferry was a base for the track forces on the middle part of the railroad. Because of this, there were at one time several section houses, one of which still stood in 2003. Photos by Barton Jennings.

A wooden boxcar was also used as employee housing at Smiths Ferry, and it was still here in 2003, but could use a new coat of paint. Photo by Barton Jennings.

**83.7** **TUNNEL NO. 5** – This is a 37-foot tunnel, reportedly the shortest solid-rock tunnel in the United States. It is built through a mass of granite, the same granite which underlies much of central Idaho.

Tunnel No. 5 is the shortest tunnel on the line, but it is also built through solid rock. For those fortunate enough to ride a passenger train through the tunnel, the views from the open bench car were thrilling. Photo by Barton Jennings.

*Idaho's Payette River Railroads: History Through the Miles*

Tunnel No. 5. Photo by Barton Jennings.

Tunnel No. 5. Photo by Barton Jennings.

**85.1 HIGHWAY 55 "RAINBOW BRIDGE"** – The railroad passes under what has been called one of the most beautiful bridges in Idaho. The highway bridge, which spans both the railroad and the North Fork Payette River, was designed by Idaho's chief bridge engineer Charles A. Kyle. Kyle grew up around bridge building as his father was superintendent of bridges for the Baltimore Bridge Company. Charles went to work at age 17, helping to replace timber railroad bridges with steel spans. He went to work for the Chicago Bridge & Iron Company through acquisition in 1889. In 1900, he began working for the American Bridge Company and managed their Lafayette, Indiana, plant. After working on a number of projects across the west, he became the Montana state bridge engineer in 1915. He took the same job in Idaho in 1919, and held that job until his death in 1936.

The Highway 55 bridge was built for $74,000 in 1933 by C. F. Dinsmore & Company, an Ogden construction firm. Funding for the bridge came from the Public Work Administration, which provided Idaho almost eight million dollars for "emergency" road projects. The bridge, originally known as the North Fork Bridge, by some as the Sunset Bridge, but by most as the Rainbow Bridge, is still Idaho's longest single-span concrete arch bridge. The bridge is 411 feet long, with the main arch span measuring 179 feet. It is listed on the National Register of Historic Places.

*Idaho Northern Branch – Emmett to Cascade*

Northbound IN&P #4506 passes under the east end of the Rainbow Bridge on a warm August day in 2003. Photo by Barton Jennings.

85.4 **ROUND VALLEY CREEK BRIDGE** – A 50-foot deck plate girder bridge is used to cross the creek, which was originally called Railroad Creek for the railroad construction camp built here. That is Round Valley just a mile to the east that Highway 55 passes through on its way to Cascade.

85.6 **HAWTHORN** – This was a 747-foot spur track used during the original track construction, later just a great place to hide a train before getting to the very busy logging area in Long Valley. There was a freight platform to the west of the tracks during the 1930s. By 1948, Hawthorn was no longer listed as a station.

89.6 **NORTH FORK PAYETTE RIVER BRIDGE** – The railroad crosses the river using a 200-foot Pratt through truss bridge. It was identified as an obstruction to men on the tops and sides of trains in a number of railroad timetables. It was also cited as a reason why the maximum class of steam locomotive on the Idaho Northern Branch was a Class 560 Consolidation (2-8-0).

Tripod Peak (8086 feet) is directly to the west and Skunk Creek Summit is to the east. Skunk Creek Summit has a number of peaks at more than 7300 feet in elevation. To the west, Fawn Creek flows into the river. Fawn Creek forms from two small streams far to the west. One branch begins in Blue Lake at an elevation of 7321 feet. The other branch forms at Hangman Tree near 7300 feet of elevation. Both are located between Granite Peak (8273 feet) and Tripod Peak. The creek flows ten miles to the southeast before flowing into the North Fork Payette River here.

The Payette River canyon has again narrowed, with just the river and railroad able to squeeze through the timber-covered mountains. Photo by Barton Jennings.

*Idaho Northern Branch – Emmett to Cascade*

Northbound IN&P #4506 crosses the North Fork Payette River bridge to move from the east bank to the west bank. Photo by Barton Jennings.

Northbound IN&P #4506 crosses the North Fork Payette River bridge. Photo by Barton Jennings.

**90.1 NAGROM** – Nagrom was another one-time logging spur that was abandoned long ago. In 1932, the track was shown to be 648 feet long. The station wasn't listed in the 1948 employee timetable.

**91.9 OLD SIDING** – This was the site of a railroad construction camp during the building of the railroad. Boise Payette Lumber Company used this site during the 1920s to load logs for movement to their sawmills. In 1940, the land along the railroad is shown as "reforestation land" owned by the Boise Payette Lumber Company.

In this area, the railroad leaves the North Fork Payette River and heads north, while the river flows in from the northeast. Heading north, the railroad enters Long Valley. The name Long Valley comes from the basic layout of the area, a long, narrow valley running north-south between the North Fork Range and Salmon River Mountains to the east and

West Mountain to the west. The valley runs between 4700 and 5000 feet of elevation while the surrounding mountains range between 7000 and 9000 feet, providing snow-capped peaks much of the year.

**92.8 CABARTON (NR)** – Cabarton has gone from being open pasture used for livestock, to being a major logging center, and then back to open pasture during the life of the railroad. As the Idaho Northern was being built northward, Boise Payette Lumber Company was created in 1913 by the merger of two Weyerhaeuser companies: Payette Lumber and Manufacturing Company and Barber Lumber. Charles (C. A.) Barton was made manager of the new organization, and he built an operations center here for the logging operations. To house the workers, 10-foot by 32-foot homes were built and mounted on skids built for easy loading on flatcars. Other camp buildings included a community bathhouse, a first-aid shack, a company store, and a roundhouse for logging locomotives, rolling stock, and horse equipment. There was also a bunkhouse and cookhouse for the single men working in the camp. A post office opened at Cabarton in 1919, but closed in 1936.

Reports state that early timber harvesting around Cabarton was done by horse skidding in conjunction with railroad hauling, and railroad spurs were pushed up most of the major stream bottoms in the area. The locomotives used by the logging railroads in this area were almost exclusively geared Shay locomotives, slow but powerful engines that could climb steep grades and make it around tight curves.

In 1914, Boise Payette built a large sawmill at Cascade, but some claim that the operations center remained at the company town of Cabarton to avoid the taxes of Cascade. C. A. Barton started several practices for the company that were reported in various logging and timber magazines of the time. He tested replanting trees on some land that they had cut, and he bought rough lumber from small mills and finished it in the Boise Payette mills. He is also credited with opening a large system of retail lumber yards in Idaho, Oregon, Wyoming and Colorado to ensure a market for the company's products.

In 1932, the railroad station at Cabarton had a 2068-foot siding, plus 1175 feet of other tracks. In 1948, Cabarton was a flag stop for the mixed passenger-freight trains. Train #385 was scheduled to be here at 3:35pm, while #386 was to be here at 9:50am. During the 1980s, Union Pacific stated that there was a 715-foot siding at 4654 feet in elevation. Heading north to Cascade, the railroad heads through the middle of Long Valley using mostly straight track.

Near Carbarton, the country opens back up with a great deal of pastureland. This view looks to the east from the railroad and towards East Mountain. Photo by Barton Jennings.

## The Public Utilities Commission of Idaho and Cabarton

While Cabarton was initially a busy place for the railroad and the Boise Payette Lumber Company, by late 1921 both were leaving the location. On September 10, 1921, the "Oregon Short Line Railroad Company, prayed that an order be made and entered authorizing and permitting the closing and discontinuance of the depot and station facilities, both passenger and freight, of an agency at Cabarton, Idaho on the grounds that the amount of business handled and transacted at said station has gradually declined until it does not now justify, warrant or render profitable or advisable for future maintenance, use or operation of the depot and station facilities, or an agency at said station; that the public convenience and necessity does not require or demand that such depot or station facilities or agency be longer continued."

In response to the request, the Public Utilities Commission of Idaho held a hearing at Cabarton on the issue. While several local farmers and ranchers protested the action, the timber company provided information that supported it. A decision was announced on October 13, 1921, that supported the closing of the agency. The information in the report provides a great deal of information about Cabarton, and resulted in a number of changes in service at the station. The following is from that report.

The evidence shows that Cabarton, Idaho is located on the Idaho Northern branch of the Oregon Short Line Railroad Company, which branch extends from Nampa, Idaho to McCall, Idaho; that Cabarton, Idaho is situated on said branch 6.1 miles east of Cascade and 10.1 miles west of Smiths Ferry, Idaho, both of which points are located on said Idaho Northern branch; that during June, 1920, a station agent was located at Cabarton on account of the large volume of business then furnished at said point by the Boise-Payette Lumber Company, who had established a logging camp at Cabarton; that the principal business transacted at said station has been freight and the principal freight business has been what is termed 'Forwarding Freight' furnished by the Boise-Payette Lumber Company and that very little freight has been received; that for a time the Boise-Payette Lumber Company shipped one train load of logs per day; that lately and during the summer of 1921 the Boise-Payette Lumber Company reduced the amount of its shipments to three trains per week and later on, or about the 25th of August, 1921; that said Boise-Payette Lumber Company notified the officials of the Oregon Short Line Railroad Company that they intended to make no more shipments of logs for the present, thereafter and during the months of September, 1921, no logs were shipped from Cabarton; that *the Boise-Payette Lumber Company is ceasing its operation at said point for the present and the said company ceasing its operation leaves but very little freight to be shipped therefrom or received at said station; that during the month of August, 1920, when the said Boise-Payette Lumber Company was operating its logging camp at Cabarton, 16 carloads of freight were received; that during the month of August, 1921, but two carloads of freight were received at Cabarton; that the prospective freight to be shipped from said point during this fall is about as follows:*

| | |
|---|---|
| *Hay* | *10 cars* |
| *Oats* | *4 cars* |
| *Timothy Seed* | *8 cars* |
| *Some Cattle* | *No. of cars unknown* |

*IT IS THEREFORE ORDERED, That the application of the Oregon Short Line Railroad Company for temporary discontinuing of station agent at Cabarton be and the same is hereby granted, to take effect on or after November 1, 1921, with the provisions that all trains stop at Cabarton, Idaho and that the station be open during the day and until the train has passed said point each way; that a stove be placed in the station and fuel be provided by the Oregon Short Line Railroad Company in or near said station for the use of passengers in order that the passengers waiting for the train may keep themselves warm; that all express or freight of every kind or nature, delivered at said point, weighing not exceeding 100 pounds be placed in the shelter of the station by the train crew immediately from the train.*

**95.3 BELVIDERE** – Belvidere is a 1485-foot siding, located just north of the Olson Creek bridge, about where the railroad curves a bit to the north. There was once a 50,000-gallon water tank here, fed from Olson Creek, that was listed as an obstruction to riders on the top and sides of trains. There was also once a freight platform to the east of the tracks, and in 1948, Belvidere was a 3:45pm flag stop for train #385, and 9:40am for train #386.

Some sources state that the station was named for a friend of the Dewey family, and sometimes spokesman for the railroad syndicate. Belvidere is at 4747 feet and in the middle of the south end of Long Valley. That is Snowbank Mountain (8322 feet) to the southwest and Collier Peak (7982 feet) to the west, both located in the Boise National Forest.

**97.0 BOISE CASCADE LOGGING RAILROAD CONNECTION** – There are a number of old logging railroad grades off to the west. Such lines once filled this valley. Today, the Cascade airport is located here to the east. The North Fork Payette River again comes next to the tracks for a short distance. Between the river and the airport is the former Cascade depot, now operated by Youth With A Mission – Idaho. Next to the depot is Union Pacific CA-9 caboose 25656. The caboose was built in August 1967 and donated in September 1989.

**99.1 CASCADE (CD)** – There is little of railroad interest today in Cascade. The sawmill is gone, so there are only a few spur tracks, a 1485-foot siding, and a wye left. There was once much more here. The railroad to Cascade was built by the Oregon Short Line after all Idaho Northern properties were sold on December 30, 1912, and in 1914 the new owner completed the remaining 45.7 miles to Lakeport, now McCall. In 1930, there was a five-pen stockyard here, plus a track section gang had section houses at Cascade. This gang maintained the track from just north of Tunnel No. 5 to here. In 1948, train #383 departed at 4:30pm for its trip on to McCall. Meanwhile, train #386 departed for Emmett at 9:30am.

Cascade was always a busy station for the railroad. Lumber and logs dominated, but ore concentrates were shipped in heavy volumes. Livestock moved in large volumes through the 1940s, and oats were regularly shipped in boxcars. The railroad had a typical two-story frame depot, located in the middle of the wye. The depot was built in 1914 and housed the station agent and family on the second floor. The depot was sold to an individual in 1986, who moved it south of town and just west of the Cascade airport on the North Fork Payette River. The depot is now part of the Youth With A Mission – Idaho facility.

Cascade is at an elevation of 4746 feet above sea level, 2599 feet above Payette. Cascade was formed in 1912 by the merger of the communities of Van Wyck, Thunder City, and Crawford when the railroad arrived in the area and bypassed the existing communities. Thunder City was founded in 1900 as a way station and outfitting post on the wagon road to the Thunder Mountain mines. The location became a ghost town when Cascade was formed next to the railroad. Van Wyck has an older history, being one of the first settlements in the area. Located west of present-day Cascade, the Van Wyck mill was here as early as 1866. By 1882 it was a small community and had a separate post office between 1888 and 1917. The Thunder Mountain mining territory is east of here and represents the last gold rush in the United States. The mines in this area also featured silver and lead. It was this mining activity and his ownership of many of the mines that interested Dewey in building a railroad into the area.

Cascade was platted in 1913 and was named for the many rapids on the North Fork of the Payette River. However, don't look for them as many were covered in 1948 by the Cascade Reservoir to the west, with a spillway height of 4828 feet. Cascade Lake is well known for fishing, waterskiing, sailing and windsurfing.

Although Cascade only has a few more than 1000 permanent residents (the number grows greatly during summer), it has a nicely restored downtown. Cascade has served as the county seat of Valley County (8000 population and named for Long Valley) since 1917 and hosts the annual Valley County Fair, with its regionally famous lumberjack competition, each August.

In 1941, a study of timber ownership in Idaho stated that there were about 81 billion feet of old growth lumber standing in Idaho. Of this, 8.8 percent was owned by the State of Idaho, 30.3 percent was privately owned, and 60.9 percent was owned by the federal government. During the latter part of the 20th Century, Boise Cascade was the largest industry and employer in the area and the only significant Idaho Northern & Pacific customer north of

Emmett until the mill closed in May 2001. However, timber has an important role in the history of Cascade, and a brief outline of this history is provided.

Sawmills have operated in Long Valley almost since the first prospector and rancher arrived. The first recognized sawmill was built and operated by Jackson Westfalls south of Cascade in 1889. In 1896, the Warren Dredge Company built the first sawmill on Payette Lake. As the railroad arrived, a number of sawmills quickly opened. Most lasted only a few years, and soon the industry was consolidated into a few major firms. For details on the various logging railroads in the Cascade area, check out the book *The Log Trains of Southern Idaho*, by Jim Witherell.

In 2003, there was still a wye at Cascade, the north end of the railroad. Here, IN&P #4506 is being turned for a trip back south on the line. This area was once full of sawmills and other timber industry buildings. Photo by Barton Jennings.

Cascade was another base of operations for the track forces, and several section buildings still stood in 2003. Photo by Barton Jennings.

This Russell Lee photograph for the U.S. Farm Security Administration shows the size of the logs that were being hauled by Union Pacific in June 1941. *Lee, Russell, photographer. Logs on flat cars at Cascade, Idaho. The state of Idaho now has about 81 billion feet of old growth lumber standing, 8.8 percent is owned by the State; 30.3 percent privately owned and 60.9 percent by the federal government. Boundary County, Cascade, Idaho. June 1941. Library of Congress. https://www.loc.gov/item/2017789940/.*

## W. H. Eccles Lumber Company

The arrival of Eccles Lumber in Cascade actually started with J. P. Dion, a logging engineer and a former Boise Payette manager, who had been fired by Weyerhaeuser in a management shakeup. In 1923, the Dion Lumber Company bought 48 million board feet of timber on Beaver and Pearsol creeks, including ponderosa pine, larch, Douglas fir, white fir, and Engelmann spruce. The firm built their mill on the east side of Cascade, near the North Fork Payette River. According to a history of the Boise National Forest, Dion Lumber built a "mill at Cascade with a daily capacity of about 50,000 board feet, built a dam, and had 3,000,000 board feet of logs in the river ready for the saw when they sold out to W. H. Eccles Lumber Company of Baker, Oregon, in 1924." In 1925, Eccles had 15 miles of logging line, two steam locomotives, and 35 flat cars used to move cut timber to the mill. Eccles Lumber had only operated here for a few years when in 1927, the Eccles Company was purchased by the Hallack & Howard Lumber Company of Denver.

For the tourist railroad or steam locomotive fan, the Cascade operations of Eccles Lumber should have some fame attached to it. W. H. Eccles Lumber Company was in the Sumpter Valley area of Oregon by 1911, operating a 3-foot gage logging railroad. In 1915, the lumber company acquired a new Heisler steam locomotive (#1306) for this operation, based upon observing similar steamers working on other area logging lines. This locomotive became Eccles #3.

In 1922, Eccles Lumber began moving much of their equipment to a new operation at Cascade. As a part of the ownership change in 1927, #3 was sold to Hallack & Howard Lumber as their #3, but never relettered. Eventually the locomotive was retired and stored in a building at the Cascade mill, being used as an auxiliary boiler. Boise Payette acquired Halleck & Howard in 1957. In 1960, the facility became part of Boise Cascade with the steam locomotive still locked up. Eventually, word got out about the Heisler and it was acquired in 1974 and moved back home to the Sumpter Valley Railroad, a steam-powered tourist operation, running trains through the Sumpter Valley area that Eccles logged.

**Hallack & Howard Lumber Company**

The Hallack & Howard Lumber Company dates back to the Hallack Brothers Lumber Company, created in 1868 by Erastus F. and Charles Hallack. The company became Hallack & Howard Lumber when Joseph H. and Charles Howard became partners in 1877. The company manufactured lumber, boxes, and even some railroad freight cars. During the early 1900s, Hallack & Howard Lumber was based in La Maderia, New Mexico. Records indicate that the company had a network of logging lines, a sawmill, planing mill, and box plant there. The company closed their New Mexico operations in 1927. The company also did some timbering by rail in southwest Colorado, with a connection to the Rio Grande Southern at Glencoe, Colorado.

On July 25, 1927, the Hallack & Howard Lumber Company acquired the Eccles Lumber Company operations at Cascade, Idaho. Over the next few years, the lumber company operated between six and ten miles of railroad. Records show that the railroad used all three types of geared logging locomotives: Shay (#1884), Heisler (#1306) and Climax (#1533).

In 1942, the Hallack & Howard Lumber Company bought 79 million board feet of timber on the South and Middle Forks of the Payette River. This was the largest sale to that date, but with labor shortages during World War II, not all of the timber was cut quickly. Hallack & Howard operated the Cascade mill until the firm was acquired by Boise Cascade in 1960, the descendent of the very firm that Dion started the mill to irritate.

Cascade meant lumber, and this June 1941 photo made by Russell Lee for the U.S. Farm Security Administration shows a lumber mill at Cascade, with a line of Union Pacific boxcars awaiting loading. Lee, Russell, photographer. Lumber mill at Cascade, Idaho. *There are about 300 lumber mills in Idaho, but 93% of the lumber is sawed by twenty-seven of these mills.* Boundary County, Cascade, Idaho. June 1941. Library of Congress. https://www.loc.gov/item/2017789971/.

### Boise Cascade

The history of Boise Cascade dates back to the early 1900s when Wyerhaeuser established the Boise Payette Lumber Company to operate in the southern Idaho area. The firm moved into this area as the Oregon Short Line built into Long Valley. The firm at first opened a branch office in Cascade and later moved their operations to Cabarton. Boise Payette became Boise Cascade in 1957 with a merger with the Cascade Lumber Company. In 1960, Boise Cascade bought the Hallack & Howard Lumber Company, gaining control of the Cascade sawmill.

Over the next four decades, the sawmill was modernized to cut smaller second growth timber, and to be more efficient with the premium old-growth logs that were sometimes obtained. However, changing timber regulations and world markets led Boise Cascade to close the mill in May 2001, ending operations in a town that gave the company half its name.

Today, the 120-acre sawmill site, including the 40-acre log yard on the south side of the property, has been cleared with the city looking for alternative uses. Part of the property is now used by Kelly's Whitewater Park, a major attraction for river users. The Cascade Aquatic and Recreation Center has also been developed on the mill site.

**99.7 END OF TRACK** – The line was abandoned north of here by Union Pacific on May 14, 1980. This was actually the second line abandoned north of here, as the construction of the Cascade Reservoir forced the railroad to a new grade in 1947.

## Idaho Northern Branch
## Cascade to McCall
### Abandoned

From Cascade to the north end of the line at McCall, the railroad has been abandoned. This part of the line was the last built and the first removed. In reality, the line between Cascade and McCall has been built twice and abandoned twice. The original construction took place in 1913-1914 by the Oregon Short Line. This line was built to serve the timber and livestock industries in Long Valley, allowing places like McCall and Donnelly to develop and grow.

By the 1940s, the North Fork of the Payette River was being considered for a series of dams, used to provide flood protection, irrigation waters, and recreation. One of these dams was to be located just north of Cascade and would flood much of the railroad in that area. In 1947, construction of the Cascade Dam was underway and approximately sixteen miles of track were relocated between Cascade and Donnelly by the U. S. Bureau of Reclamation.

On September 2, 1942, Union Pacific had applied to abandon some of the track and construct new track to stay above the waters of Lake Cascade. As reported by the Interstate Commerce Commission: "Application of Oregon Short Line Railroad Company for authority to abandon a portion of a branch line of railroad known as the Idaho-Northern Branch in Valley County, Idaho a distance of 9.37 miles and for the Union Pacific Railroad Company to abandon operation thereover and for the former to acquire and latter company to operate a line of railroad to be constructed in Valley County, Idaho by The United States of

America in the same general direction approx. 1½ miles away from the present track and approx. 4.15 miles longer than the existing line."

The request to abandon part of the railroad was due to the start of the construction on the dam in 1942, but it was delayed by World War II. Construction began again in 1946 and was completed in 1948. A contract between Union Pacific and the federal government stated that "The United States shall, at its sole cost and expense....acquire and convey, or cause to be conveyed, to the Railroad Company, its successors and assigns, by good and sufficient deed or deeds in fee simple," the real property required for the relocation of the railroad line. In other words, Union Pacific swapped the old flooded line for a newer line above the new lake level.

**The Original Line**

The original rail line to McCall crossed the North Fork Payette River on the north side of Cascade, just upstream of the highway bridge. The route then made a horseshoe curve to follow the river along the east bank. Where it reached the original route of State Highway 15, it turned north, running just off of the west shoulder of the road. The railroad continued straight when the road curved a bit to the east, passing through Timothy. Almost immediately after crossing Hot Spring Creek, the railroad turned due north, passing through Arling and MacGregor, and then turned slightly northwest just south of Donnelly. The railroad passed along the west side of Donnelly and headed to Norwood. North of Norwood, the railroad turned more to the northwest. Near the Payette River, the railroad made several turns and headed northeast, before turning back north to enter McCall. At McCall, the railroad went up the southeast corner of Payette Lake a short distance to where there was a wye track at the Brown Tie & Lumber Company facility.

Some information about the stations lost with the construction of the new line would be appropriate. In 1932, there was an 811-foot spur track at **Tie Spur (Milepost 100.8)**, plus a freight platform to the west of the tracks. At the time, many ties were cut in the hills and floated down the various parts of the Payette River. There was a tie mill that cut the timber to size in this area.

The station of **Timothy (Milepost 104.2)** no longer exists as it is under approximately fifty feet of water. It was located to the southwest of today's Sugarloaf Campground. In 1932, there was a 336-foot spur track here, and it was still shown as a station on a 1940 county map. The property to the west belonged to the Cruickshank family, while the property to the east was owned by the Center Irrigation District.

The name Timothy is important to the Long Valley area of Idaho, as this is one of the few areas in the United States where Timothy grass seed is grown commercially. Timothy has been described as a relatively short-lived, cool-season perennial that grows in erect clumps 20 to 40 inches tall, and has a shallow, compact, and fibrous root system. It grows best in rich, moist bottomlands, especially in a cool and humid climate, but not in standing water. Timothy is very winter hardy and has high tolerance to cold temperatures and ice encasement. It is favored for livestock production and is used mainly for hay, but also for pasture and silage. It is palatable and nutritious, and makes an excellent companion grass for alfalfa, trefoil, or clover since it does not compete with legumes. Producing the seed can be complicated because there are approximately 1,152,000 seeds per pound. Sources from the 1920s and 1930s stated that "The timothy meadows of Long Valley Idaho can produce two to four tons of hay per acre, or 300 to 600 pounds of seed per acre."

In addition to these stations, the railroad station and community at **Arling** was flooded, but a new Arling siding was built on higher ground to the east of the lake. Some track to the north toward Donnelly was also simply raised to stay above the higher waters.

The new line was longer, but in better condition than the original line. Train times did not change significantly, even with the longer route. However, after the Boise Cascade sawmill closed in McCall in October of 1977, there was no freight traffic beyond Cascade. Therefore, on May 14, 1980, the line beyond Cascade was abandoned again.

The following route description covers the new line built in the 1940s. The telegraph code for each station, as shown in the *Union Pacific System List of Officers, Agencies, Stations, Etc. No. 60*, dated January 1, 1930, is included with the station name.

**99.7 END OF TRACK** – The line was abandoned north of here by Union Pacific on May 14, 1980. This was actually the second line abandoned north of here, as the construction of the Cascade Reservoir forced the railroad to a new grade in 1947.

The "new" line, built in the 1940s and officially opened on July 3, 1947, was all new south of Donnelly, where the valley was covered by Lake Cascade. The rail line north of Donnelly was kept and used until the line was abandoned entirely north of Cascade. The challenge for the 1940s line was to gain elevation to stay above the lake. To do this, the railroad crossed the North Fork Payette River and followed Highway 55 to the northeast. At today's highway maintenance facility, the railroad made a tight 180-degree turn to head back towards the river, but at a higher elevation. The railroad grade then ran along the hillside just above the lake, with the grade now used as Vista Point Boulevard, and then the Crown Point Trail. The railroad grade eventually becomes Hall Lane, and then turns north as a simple grade through pasture land. The grade comes next to Idaho Highway 55 at Stonebreaker Lane. Both the old railroad grade and Highway 55 head north through the relocated Arling location, before the railroad grade curves northwest and crosses Hot Spring Creek. The new line rejoined the original line just south of Down End Way.

**Crown Point Trail**

This trail currently covers 2.7 miles of the abandoned railroad grade along the east shore of Lake Cascade. The south end is at the Crown Point Parkway entrance to the Crown Point Campground, a part of Lake Cascade State Park. There are plans to extend the trail northward for ten miles, but agreements with landowners for rights across their properties have not yet been reached.

The trail is popular for wildlife viewing as osprey, bald eagle, foxes, wolf, cougar, deer, raccoons, badgers, and black bears have all been seen, or at least their prints have been seen, along the route. There are also some interpretive signs along the trail. The trail is used for both summer and winter recreation.

During the past decade, there have been several efforts to turn the entire Cascade to McCall right-of-way into a trail. There has been some success, but much of the route was sold to developers and local ranchers, and dozens of houses now stand where trains once operated.

**99.8   NORTH FORK PAYETTE RIVER BRIDGE** – The railroad crossed the river using a steel deck plate girder span. Note that there are two sets of headwalls here; the ones for the original route and then the ones for the 1940s route. It is interesting to note that the original headwalls are still in service. The 98-foot deck plate girder span from 1915 is now used as a road bridge for Lake Way.

**101.2   HORSESHOE CURVE** – The railroad made a tight curve here, changing from heading northeast to heading southwest. The curve also gained more than fifty feet in elevation as it climbed the side of the ridge known as Crown Point.

**111.0   ARLING** – When the Cascade Dam and Reservoir was built, Arling was one of several communities flooded. Before the construction of the lake, the 1645-foot siding was at Milepost 108.1. The new Arling was built on higher ground to the east, which also had a siding as well as a three-pen stockyard. In 1948, train #385 could be flagged here at 5:00pm, while #386 could be flagged at 8:00am.

   A map from 1940 shows Arling to the west of the tracks and consisting of thirteen blocks of stores and houses. There was a post office at the original Arling from 1915 until 1941. The post office played a major role in the name of the community, as it was originally Arlington, but the post office shortened it to Arling to avoid a conflict with the name of several other post offices in the region. Today, the tracks are gone, the railroad grade is just west of Highway 55, and a few hay sheds mark the location.

**115.4 GOLD FORK RIVER BRIDGE** – The 1940s railroad used the same grade as the original line in this area, but it required a long fill and a bridge to cross the river, which became a part of Lake Cascade after the dam was built. Gold Fork River forms in the mountains to the east, about sixteen miles away, at an elevation of 5235 feet.

**116.9 MACGREGOR** – MacGregor was a short-lived logging town operated by Boise Payette Lumber Company, located at Milepost 112.8 on the pre-Cascade Dam line. When the lumber ran out south of Cascade, the town of Cabarton was picked up and moved to here in 1935. There was a post office at MacGregor from 1936 until 1940. The land to the east was owned by Boise Payette Lumber and the Idaho Northern had a railroad spur in that direction for several years. The name MacGregor honors Boise Payette Lumber Company superintendent Gordon MacGregor. Early timetables show that this was actually the second MacGregor station on the Idaho Northern Branch. In a 1928 timetable, there was a MacGregor station at Milepost 81.0.

MacGregor was located not far south of Loomis Lane, which the spur track followed to the east. The railroad grade in this area is now occupied by houses.

**119.4 DONNELLY (DN)** – While the town of Donnelly did not move, its milepost changed with the construction of the Cascade Dam. Its original milepost was 115.3, when there was a 1780-foot siding and a 456-foot spur track. There was also a freight platform for smaller shipments, located to the west of the track. In 1930, Donnelly had a 50,000-gallon water tank fed by a well, a two-pen stockyard, and a section gang responsible for the track between mileposts 99.3 and 114.8. In 1948, train #385 was scheduled to depart Donnelly at 5:30pm, while train #386 departed at 7:35am. The livestock business apparently grew as by 1951 the stockyard had been enlarged to four pens.

The first settlements on the valley floor near where Donnelly developed were made by squatters, and the first town was located several miles east of here. A store and post office opened there in 1892 with Lewis Roseberry as the first postmaster, giving the town the name Roseberry. It became a supply post for area mines and ranches, and was soon the largest community in the Long Valley region. The town of Spink was located three miles north of Roseberry with Mrs. Lydia Spink as postmaster. Both towns were impacted by the construction of the Idaho Northern Railway.

When the railroad built to the west, many businesses and residents moved to be near the railroad. Some of these people brought their own buildings over from Roseberry, including the First State Bank building that still stands at Jordan and Main Streets. The original plat of Donnelly had three east-west streets named State Street, Jordan Street and Roseberry Road from north to south. There were four north-south running streets: Front Street (immediately east of the railroad), Main Street, Commercial Street, and Payette Street, listed from west to east. Main Street is today Idaho Highway 55.

In the town's original design, the depot was on the west side of the mainline (between it and the siding to the west) at the west end of State Street. As the town became established, the estate of Colonel

Dewey donated more land in 1914 to allow the community to grow. The City of Donnelly was incorporated in 1914 and a post office opened at Donnelly the same year, and the community hit its peak population in 1916 at about 200 residents.

The name Donnelly comes from Mr. Peter Donnelly, who was an employee and friend of Colonel Dewey. When founded, ranching and timber supported the City of Donnelly, but today recreation and tourism have a big impact upon the community. The post office is still open and the population was 152 at the 2010 census.

**122.2 LAKE FORK BRIDGE** – The bridges in this area were of timber construction, typically pile trestles. Lake Fork forms to the northeast and flows generally to the southwest before entering Lake Cascade in the Lake Cascade Wildlife Management Area. There is a small unincorporated community along the stream known as Lake Fork, the site of a number of gravel pits. Most histories of the area state that the area was heavily settled by families from Finland, who came here because it was similar to their original homes.

**124.7 NORWOOD** – Norwood was another railroad station that was not changed by the construction of the Cascade Dam and Reservoir; however, its mileposts did change. Before the dam, Norwood was at Milepost 120.6, later it was at Milepost 124.7 as 4.15 miles of track was added to avoid the lake.

In 1932, Norwood was an 819-foot siding with a freight platform to the east of the tracks. There was a one-pen stockyard in 1930, which was expanded to two pens by 1951. Train #385 was a 5:45pm flag stop at Norwood, while train #386 could be flagged at 7:22am. There was a Norwood post office 1915-1941. Today, Norwood is a small community that features stockyards as well as the Cruzen Ditch. Norwood Road follows the railroad grade closely to the east.

The Cruzen Ditch was built by the Cruzen Irrigation District, and named for the Cruzen Ranch. The ranch was operated for generations by the Cruzen family, first growing timothy seed, and then handling livestock grazing. Eddie Cruzen was the subject of a Farm Security Administration study during the late 1930s and early 1940s about ranching practices in the area. Maps show that Stella Cruzen owned land here and to the south in 1940.

**127.6 ARCHABAL** – This station was once at the Heinrich Lane grade crossing at an elevation of 5002 feet. The station was known as Chrisman in 1930, and featured an eight-pen stockyard that year. However, the stockyards were gone by 1951. There was also once a freight platform to the west of the tracks. In 1948, Archabal was shown as a flag stop, but no times were provided.

**North Valley Rail Trail**

From Archabal to 3rd Avenue and Park Street in downtown McCall, the former right-of-way of the Idaho Branch is generally used by the North Valley Rail Trail, for a distance of 5.9 miles. Heading north from Archabal, the railroad grade curves to the northwest, and the grade is clearly visible as it stays to the north of Hogue Hollow Road. The grade follows Hogue Hollow Road to make a turn to the northeast, winding around new housing. The grade then follows Moonridge Drive to the south and east, which once served as part of the McCall Corporate Limits. The railroad once continued to the northeast, crossing Mission Road just north of the intersection with River Ranch Road. The railroad then turned north. Here, the grade is now used as the west taxiway for the McCall Municipal Airport.

The railroad grade heads due north from the airport, and then curves to the northeast to reach the southeast corner of Payette Lake, where various sawmills existed for decades, and where the railroad's yard and shop facilities once stood. The part of the trail north of the airport is paved while the right-of-way to the south is still dirt.

Where the railroad grade crosses Stibnite Street, maps from 1940 show that the property to the west of the tracks belonged to the Brown Tie & Lumber Company. The railroad turned to the northeast and crossed just north of the 3rd Avenue and Park Street intersection, where the North Valley Rail Trail ends. The railroad once continued through what is today parking lots until it reached the mill and wye track at today's Brown Park, located along Payette Lake.

**McCall Smokejumper Base**

On the west side of the McCall Municipal Airport is the U.S. Forest Service McCall Smokejumper Base, one of only four Forest Service smokejumper training bases in the United States, and one of seven national bases for smokejumpers. The McCall complex includes a smokejumper training unit, paraloft, the Payette National Forest dispatch office and the McCall air tanker base. During the summer fire season, there are 70 smokejumpers, 3 smokejumper aircraft and 2 air tankers based here. There is also a Helibase here.

The idea of smokejumping was first proposed in 1934. The idea came from T. V. Pearson, the U.S. Forest Service Intermountain Regional Forester. The idea was to speed the movement of fire-fighting resources to the fire before it got too big. At first the idea was rejected, but was proved successful when tested in 1939-1940 in the Pacific Northwest Region, with the first successful fire jump made in Idaho's Nez Perce National Forest. Several information signs are located here and tours are sometimes available of the facility.

**132.8 McCALL (NE)** – The history of McCall begins long before the first building was erected. The area was first used for hunting and fishing by a number of native tribes, most famously the Tukudeka, or Sheep Eaters, a branch of the Shoshone. They occupied the higher mountain valleys in the region, and didn't leave this area until the late 1870s when miners and ranchers discovered the valley's riches. Some of the early miners searched the shores of Payette Lake, located at the head of Long Valley, hoping to find a source of gold.

In 1874, Norman Bushnell Willey, later the second Governor of Idaho (1890-1893), wrote a number of stories about Long Valley and Payette Lake for several newspapers. Among his writing was the statement "Payette Lake, a beautiful sheet of water 12 miles long, in places is dotted with richly wooded inlets set like emerald gems on the bosom of the liquid mirror." While no town immediately developed, commercial fishing did get started to feed area miners. The construction of several roads to serve mines, mail and freight haulers led to the construction of a number of buildings at the south end of Lake Payette.

In 1889, today's McCall was one house and one settler – Sam Devers, who had claimed squatter's rights to 160 acres of prime shoreline property. He traded his land and cabin to Tom and Louisa McCall in exchange for a wagon, team and harness. The McCall family had left Ohio for a new start and challenge, and they saw a future in the land at the south end of Payette Lake. Their work attracted other settlers, and Tom McCall plotted a four-block town site. To support the town, Tom McCall also claimed the abandoned Lardo post office, once located ten miles south of the lake, on September 19, 1894.

A number of other local communities were founded by Finnish settlers who created sober restrictions for their farming towns. However, McCall served miners, loggers and teamsters, and became known for its gambling, dance halls, drinking and lakeside whorehouses. The McCall family took advantage of the attractions, and opened a hotel and general store. They also contracted with the Warren Gold Dredging Company sawmill to cut lumber that they then sold.

Despite the growth of McCall's town, the Lardo post office was acquired by W. B. Boydstun on January 12, 1903, and moved to his homestead, located on the west side of the North Fork Payette River. After the Cole family took charge of the Lardo post office in 1912, it lasted only a few more years before being discontinued on October 15, 1917, with mail service being moved to McCall. A second post office opened about a mile to the south on March 31, 1905, using the name Elo. This post office was soon moved north and was renamed McCall.

Tom McCall took other actions to make his town a success. He invested in a sawmill, which he bought from Warren Dredging and later sold to the Hoff & Brown Lumber Company. Several tourist hotels and recreational facilities were built to encourage visitors to the lake. Tom also saw an opportunity when the Payette Forest Reserve was created in 1905 by President Theodore Roosevelt. He provided office space and paid for the supervisor and his family to move from their original headquarters at Meadow to McCall. About the same time, a number of timber companies formed the Southern Idaho Timber Protective Association (SITPA) to jointly protect area forests from fire, disease, and other destructive practices. This organization was also encouraged to locate in McCall, and their headquarters, built by the Civilian Conservation Corps during the 1930s, still stands on State Street. The building currently houses the Central Idaho Historical Museum and is on the National Register of Historic Places.

Tom McCall was recognized by many as the founder and father of the town, and it was made official on July 19, 1911, when the Village of McCall was officially incorporated. However, there were some issues when the railroad arrived. The Oregon Short Line opened their railroad to McCall on July 19, 1914. The end of the railroad was actually north of McCall, and the railroad named their station Lakeport. This caused a battle of names for a while as postal officials refused to create a new Lakeport post office, and the Town of McCall refused to change its name. Within a year, the railroad gave up and moved their office to where the depot was eventually built, and renamed the station McCall.

Despite the issues that the name battle caused, the railroad did make McCall a regional commercial center. Mining, timber and livestock all became important for the community, and the railroad. Tourism was also important, and the creation of the Winter Carnival in 1924 has led to a 10-day event that now attracts 50,000 visitors each year. In 1938, McCall got national attention as the movie *Northwest Passage* was filmed here, starring Spencer Tracy, Robert Young, and Walter Brennan.

Despite the loss of the timber industry, McCall has continued to grow as a tourism destination. A number of developments have pumped money into the area, and the population grew from 2084 (2000 census) to 2991 in the 2010 census. Today, McCall features marinas, museums, and a 27-hole golf course. There are also numerous restaurants and hotels. For those wanting more information about the history of the community, there are a number of interpretive signs throughout downtown McCall.

**The Timber Industry**

Timber was cut in the late 1800s to build cabins and support mines. The first major sawmill was built and operated by the Warren Gold Dredging Company. Tom McCall was soon involved with the sawmill, and in 1910, Hans Hoff and his son Theodore Hoff created the Hoff Company and acquired the sawmill. To provide logs for the sawmill, a number of log docks were built along the north end of Payette Lake, especially around North Beach. There, logs were dragged by ox and mule teams to the docks, the logs dumped in the lake and floated to the mill at McCall. Property maps also show that the Boise Payette Lumber Company had property in the area, especially around the river near Lardo.

In 1914, with contracts to deliver ties to the railroad, Hoff & Brown Tie Company was created. The firm later became the Brown Tie & Lumber Company when Carl Brown bought out the Hoff family, which operated the sawmill until it was sold to Boise Cascade in 1964. For years, this mill was the heart of the McCall timber business, but the last log went through the Boise Cascade mill during October 1977. Soon after, Union Pacific ended service to McCall, and the tracks were removed in 1980.

The Brown Tie & Lumber Company Mill and Burner was placed on the National Register of Historic Places on December 20, 1978. However, the sawmill burned to the ground in 1984 and it was officially removed from the list on January 31, 1986. The Murray-Corliss engine which powered the Brown Tie & Lumber Company mill from 1940-1983 can now be viewed at the Central Idaho Cultural Center and Museum at 1001 State Street. Today, the site of the sawmill and log docks are used by Brown Park, the local marina, and new homes.

**The Railroad**

Because McCall was the end of the line, and most trains covered the route in only one direction in a day, the Oregon Short Line built a number of rail facilities at McCall. For the locomotives, there was a 2-stall engine house, built with 79-foot-long stalls. There was no turntable, instead a wye was used to turn the locomotives and passenger cars.

A 50,000-gallon water tank was located here which used Payette Lake as its source. A Union Pacific document stated that there was one water column in the yard that was used to water the locomotives. Finally, there was a 40-ton coal dock platform with an air hoist to fuel the steam locomotives. This coal dock was retired after oil-burning steam locomotives began to be used on the line in 1941.

Besides the shop and servicing facilities, the railroad also had several section houses for the track maintenance gang that took care of the track from McCall to near Donnelly. Despite the fact that logs and lumber was the dominant traffic on the line, other products did move, and the railroad had facilities for them, too. In 1951, the railroad had an 8-pen stockyard to move regular shipments of livestock. There was also a freight platform on the west side of the tracks for general freight shipments. All of the switching that was done required more than 4500 feet of yard and spur tracks, in addition to the 2473-foot siding.

The McCall depot was somewhat unique in that it was a one-story frame building, originally located near 3rd Avenue and East Lake Street. In 1948, train #385 was scheduled to arrive at McCall at 6:15pm to end its journey. Train #386 was scheduled to depart at 7:00am, both scheduled for daily except Sunday service. The depot, after being closed, was sold and moved in the early 1980s to 411 Railroad Avenue. The depot has since been used by a series of restaurants and breweries. Nearby is what is reported to be the former railroad stationmaster's house.

*Idaho's Payette River Railroads: History Through the Miles*

## About the Author

For almost three decades, Barton Jennings has been organizing charter passenger trains and writing the route descriptions, both for planning purposes and for the enjoyment of the passengers. These trips have been from coast to coast, often covering operations that haven't seen a passenger train in decades. For example, he chartered a passenger train over the entire Idaho Northern & Pacific route from Payette to Cascade in August 2003.

In addition, he has written a number of articles about various railroads for rail hobby magazines. His basement has several rooms full of books, timetables and other documents about this and other railroads – important research items from a time long before today's internet. Today, Bart Jennings, after years working in the railroad industry, is a professor emeritus of supply chain management and teaches transportation operations. He also still teaches regulatory issues for the railroad industry, a way to stay in touch with the industry he loves.

*Idaho's Payette River Railroads: History Through the Miles*

www.ingramcontent.com/pod-product-compliance
Lightning Source LLC
Chambersburg PA
CBHW071451080526
44587CB00014B/2071